# A
# BOOK
## OF
# CATS

An illustration from the supplement to *Harpers Weekly* supplement, 27 January 1872, an illustration of several feline exhibits from the London Crystal Palace show.

# A
# BOOK
## OF
# CATS

## LITERARY, LEGENDARY AND HISTORICAL

### DOROTHY M. STUART

FONTHILL

Fonthill Media Limited
Fonthill Media LLC
www.fonthillmedia.com
office@fonthillmedia.com

First published in the United Kingdom
and the United States of America 2015

British Library Cataloguing in Publication Data:
A catalogue record for this book is available from the British Library

ISBN 978-1-78155-490-6

Typeset in 10.5pt on 13pt Sabon
Printed and bound by CPI Group (UK) Ltd, Croydon, CR0 4YY

# Contents

Publisher's Note                                                           7

1  In Ancient Egypt, Greece and Rome                         9

2  Some Celtic and Medieval Cats                                 25

3  Tudor and Shakespearean Cats                                 42

4  The Witch's Familiar—More Literary Cats              55

5  Dr Johnson—Horace Walpole—Thomas Gray—

   Christopher Smart—Cat-lovers All                            71

6  Some Augustan and Regency Cats                             88

7  A few Victorian and Post-Victorian Cats                 106

   Endnotes                                                                126

Henry Wriothesley, 3rd Earl of Southampton, in the Tower of London in 1603, attributed to John de Critz.

# Publisher's Note

Dorothy Margaret Stuart, (1889-1963) was a poet and writer of great ability. Her works include literary and historical biographies, historical non-fiction particularly concentrating on the lives of women and children, and history stories for children. She was a member of the English Association from 1930 onwards, edited its newsletter and contributed essays and book reviews to its journal, *English*.

In *A Book of Cats* we find her at her most whimsical, and clearly a cat lover she wrote the book out of pure affection. A great scholar and linguist, she assumes that her readers will also be people of intellect. Therefore, a slight warning note should be sounded inasmuch as a good knowledge of history (especially English and Scottish history) and English Literature will make the book far more understandable.

Notwithstanding the numerous literary allusions, most cat lovers will find her text entertaining and will reflect on the fact that the cat's nature has not changed over the centuries.

This work was first published in 1959. No attempt has been made to update it as such a task is not only unnecessary, but pointless. It should therefore be borne in mind that when she refers to events as contemporaneous, they are in fact of some sixty years ago.

One final point, the quote the author was searching for in chapter 7 was by Winston Churchill: 'I am fond of pigs. Dogs look up to us. Cats look down on us. Pigs treat us as equals.'

The Gayer-Anderson cat, representing the Egyptian goddess Bastet.

1

# In Ancient Egypt, Greece and Rome

It was from Libya that she made her way into the land of Egypt and into the homes and the temples of the Ancient Egyptians. Aloof, graceful, of unfailing dignity, with mysterious expanding and contracting eyes to which the darkness was not dark, she would have been an obvious candidate for deification even among a people less apt to integrate their animals with their gods. Beauty was not demanded of these sacred beasts. Nobody could have called Ta-urt, the hippopotamus-headed wife of Set, even moderately good-looking. And the dog's head of Anubis was a hideous, grinning head. But the two goddesses, Ubastet (otherwise Bastet, ultimately Bast) and Sekmet, who wore feline masks wore them with a difference. Whether it be in the likeness of a lioness or of a cat the mask could never be described as ugly, for all the bristling whiskers and the slightly sinister slant of the eye.

More ancient than either was yet another cat-goddess, Mafdet, who appears as early as the First Dynasty in the act of protecting Pharaoh's house from snakes. In a Twelfth Dynasty tomb at Abydos, Flinders Petrie found seventeen skeletons of cats; in the recess intended for offerings stood a row of the roughest little votive pots, presumably meant to contain milk.

As the long sequence of centuries dawned and darkened over the Nile Valley the cult of the cat-goddess established itself ever more firmly there. It would last well into the Roman period.

Bast typified the kindly, fructifying powers of the sun: she was the Lady of Life, the Soul of Osiris, the Eye of Ra. Her 'opposite number', Sekmet, symbolized his destructive power and wore the features of a lioness. Yet it must be confessed that these two divine ladies sometimes tended to melt into each other after the disconcerting fashion of heathen gods. Each could, if she chose, poise the sun's disc or the sacred uraeus upon her shallow brows; but it is curious that the amiable Bast should have cared to assume the face of the unamiable Sekmet, as she seems occasionally to have done.

Whether she was represented as having a human body with a cat's head or as being incarnate in the complete body of a cat depended upon time, place and religious fashion. The Greeks, the Hellenized Egyptians and the Romans identified her with Artemis or Diana. 'When the gods', wrote Ovid, 'fled into Egypt and hid themselves there under borrowed forms, the sister of Apollo wore the similitude of a cat.' He does not say that she wore the *head* of a cat.

In her heyday Bast was the honoured patroness of the eastern half of the Delta. The centre of her cult was at Per-Ubastet, the 'Bubastis' of Herodotus, in the district now known as Beni-Hassan. Modern archaeologists exploring the site discovered that the mound into which they delved was called Tell-Basta. Centuries of Islamic domination had not robbed the cat-goddess of her ninth life.

The Goddess Bastet, with Sistrum, Ægis and Kittens. *British Museum*

To the Jewish prophets all this bowing down to graven images was most repugnant; and the ineradicable tendency of their people to 'go a-whoring after strange gods' must have lent a sharper edge to their fury. Bubastis, under the name of 'Pi-Beseth', is mentioned in one of the most minatory passages in the Book of the Prophet Ezekiel, where he foretells with a certain grim glee the downfall and desolation of the idolatrous land of Egypt.

Bast received especial honours from the Libyan Pharaohs of the Twenty-Second Dynasty, who were in a sense her compatriots. To this period belongs the delightful bronze figurine in the British Museum where she is shown with large, pricked up ears and wears upon her human body a long, close-fitting garment embroidered with a reticular design and scored with perpendicular stripes. One hand holds the sistrum, the sacred rattle so much used in religious rites, and the other a sort of *pochette* known as her *aegis*.[1] Both objects are ornamented with cat-masks. In the Hermetic Books anciently ascribed to Hermes Trismegistus, otherwise the god Thoth, it is stated that this mask symbolizes the moon, 'on account of the cat's variable nature, nocturnal habits and fecundity': and it seems strange that the Egyptians should have elected to associate Bast with the sun to the exclusion of the moon, who also has what may justly be described as nocturnal habits and a variable nature.

At the feet of the figurine described above sit four charming kittens. These little creatures often appear, with or without their divine mother, in the art of Ancient Egypt. They played a part analogous to that of the *amorini* in Baroque sculpture; they introduce a note almost of gaiety. One finds them on sistra, on sceptre-heads, in amulets of carved crystal, in vivid blue or green faience, even as beads in royal necklaces.

Votive images of cats are usually naturalistic: sometimes a relaxed pose is copied straight from nature: sometimes the animal sits erect, as she so often does in real life, front paws close together, tail primly curved round them. Eyes are inlaid with obsidian, rock-crystal, lapis-lazuli, even with gold. The ears, or even the nose, may be pierced for rings. In some instances these adornments still exist. Collars and necklaces encircled furry necks; these may have been personal trinkets, not any part of a cult offering.

The yearly festival of the cat-headed sun-goddess was held in the spring, when tokens of her unchanging beneficence were everywhere visible. It was, as the late Dr James Baikie gravely observed, 'something in the nature of a bean-feast'. The rowdy element, seldom absent on such occasions, was much in evidence at Bubastis. According to Herodotus more grape-wine was then drunk than in the whole of the years besides.

When seven thousand pilgrims assembled, playing flutes, singing sometimes indecorous songs, eating and drinking, dancing, indulging in boisterous jests and even more boisterous horseplay, the result must have been anything rather than edifying. Some of the visitors would take boats and, paddling as near as possible to the reedy margin of the water, would bandy quips with the crowds on the shore. In this light-hearted exchange women seem to have borne a leading part, as befitted the votaresses of a female divinity.

It seems paradoxical that all this uncouth, noisy fun should have been linked with the image of a cat, an animal who, however playful she may on occasion condescend to be, never stoops to the awkward gambols in which a dog will quite unselfconsciously indulge.

By some persuasion of their own the Egyptians overcame the cat's inherited repugnance towards water, her proverbial reluctance to wet her delicate paws. When some great one, a scribe of Pharaoh's household or a captain of his chariots, went fowling with a throw-stick he often used a trained cat to retrieve the birds as, dazed or dying, they fluttered down among the blue-blossomed papyrus reeds.

A Saite 26th Dynasty period (664-525 BC) bronze art work of an Egyptian cat playing with one of her kittens and feeding another. *Gulbekian Museum*

Such a scene is shown on several surviving tomb-paintings. There is a well-known example in the British Museum. The hunter, wigged, necklaced, girt with a loin-cloth of fine linen, stands erect in the act of aiming his snake-shaped stick. His womenkind are with him—the Ancient Egyptian equivalent of 'going out with the guns'. His wife, upright in the stern, poises on her head, above the wig, one of those cones of nard which by slowly dissolving were supposed to give comfort in hot weather: his small daughter, with shaven skull and exiguous costume, grasps him firmly by the leg. A single glance at the highly competent retrieving cat is enough to prove that she approached her duties without any reluctance. She has succeeded in seizing three birds at once, one with her hind paws, one with her forepaws, one in her mouth. Her coat is of a tawny brown handsomely striped with tabby markings. In the water beneath the canoe fish teem: in the sky above butterflies flutter. Such would be the scenes and the delights which the stick-throwing gentleman confidently expected to find in the world to come, where his faithful cat would bear him company.

In another wall-painting, hardly less charming, one of the ladies tethers the canoe by clutching a handful of reeds while the cat, beautifully striped and very life-like, rears up in an attitude of supplication, as if saying, 'Oh, pray, can I not get on with my job?'

Her voice, as conveyed by her Egyptian name, must have been very similar to the voice of the cats of today. That name was *Mau*. When out hunting she would perforce doff her immemorial dignity, but she might not have been pleased if she had known that a tomb-painter had caught her in either a pouncing or an imploring pose. Still less would she have liked to see herself in a 'comic-strip' papyrus, walking along on her hind legs, a stick grasped in one paw, and driving before her a gaggle of anxious-looking geese.

The *Mau* was a domestic pet as well as a goddess and a huntress, and in that character also she is always what Miss Austen would have called 'quite the lady'. Usually she arranges both paws and tail as if in obedience to some feline code of deportment; at other times she hastily devours a fish or a duck beneath the dinner-table, yet never with any real loss of dignity. In the Cairo Museum there is a carved chair-back which shows Queen Tiye, wife of Amenophis III, taking her pleasure on the water in a narrow skiff; with two fan-waving damsels (one of them a princess) at prow and stern. Under the Queen's chair, cosy and condescending, sits her pet cat.

This queen, Tiye, was the mother of Akhenaton, the Heretic Pharaoh, whose efforts to introduce a monotheistic religion into the most madly polytheistic country in the antique world brought him to destruction. She was not Egyptian-born and it may have been that the Great Heresy was derived indirectly from her lack of enthusiasm for the teeming gods which bedevilled her adopted country.

Tiye had a brother, Onen by name, the walls of whose tomb at Thebes bear the likeness of a cat conjecturally identified with his royal sister's favourite. Of course the lively animal devouring a goose beneath his chair may have been one of his own: but at a later date, when the reaction against Akhenaton was in full swing, the head of this cat was deliberately erased. The close connection between the cat, who could claim kinship with the Aton, the sun-symbol of the One God, may have accounted for the erasure, even if she were not recognizably Queen Tiye's particular pet; but it is remarkable that the goose, sacred to Amon-Ra, should have been left untouched. The monotheistic Aton-sun was taboo, while the Amon-Ra sun blazed in triumph over a vast and varied pantheon; nor is there any indication that Bast fell under suspicion because of her solar affiliations.

Cats must have been permitted—even encouraged—to live, mate and breed in the temple courts of Bubastis; and according to the prophet Baruch they also invaded the sacred places of Babylon. With vehemence he sets forth the folly of those who put their trust in impotent idols incapable of protecting themselves from moth and rust, 'though they be covered with purple raiment', and whose faces have to be wiped clean from the dust of the temple 'when there is much upon them'. These carven faces, blurred by dust, blackened by smoke, were further befouled by bats, swallows and various birds perching on their bodies and heads, 'and the cats also'. Alice's drowsy question, 'Do cats eat bats?' might well have found its answer in the temples of Babylon.

When we make the obvious transition from Ancient Egypt to Ancient Greece we find a curious dearth of cats. It has been suggested that one of their Greek names, *ailouros*, may have been derived from two words, *ailos*, swift, changing, and *oura*, a tail, 'as expressive of the wavy motion of the tail peculiar to the cat-kind'. The other name was *galen*, but unfortunately this is shared between the cat and the weasel, and some ambiguity follows. Both beasts are sworn foes to mice, and were employed as mice-exterminators in Greek households, but one might have expected the logical Attic mind to draw a clear terminological line

Detail of cat from the hunting scene (fowling scene) from the tomb of Nebamun, Thebes, Egypt, 18th dynasty, *c.* 1400-1350 BC.

between them. A myth of rather late emergence relates how Galinthias, one of the daughters of Proteus, legendary King of Egypt, was changed into a *galen*. Hecate had compassion upon her and made her a priestess. The twofold link with witchcraft and with Egypt suggests that in this instance the word indicated a cat and not a weasel.

The Greeks were not cat-conscious. Their only famous poet to allude to 'the cat-kind' was Theocritus, and he was a Syracusan not a Greek by birth. Also the allusion occurs once only. It is in his fifth Idyll, recording the lively colloquy between Gorgo and Praxinoë, two ladies of Syracuse. Praxinoë, impatient at the awkward fumbling of her slave-girl, flings at her what seems to be a proverbial saying: 'Cats like to sleep soft.' *Galen* must in this context mean a cat and not a weasel. During the time that the poet spent at the court of Ptolemy Philadelphus at Alexandria he would have seen many a cherished royal *Mau* 'sleeping soft' on a bed of blue and purple linen.

Though the days of Egypt's glory had departed when Herodotus sojourned there in the fifth century BC, the cult of the cat still flourished as it had continued to do while Macedonian, Greek and Persian conquerors filled the throne of the vanished Pharaohs, and would continue to do after the land became a Roman province.

By the time that the Father of History visited Bubastis the integration of Bast with Artemis was so complete that he could write of the great festivals held there in honour of the Moon-Goddess of the Greeks without even mentioning the feline sun-goddess of the Egyptians. Faithful to his rule of eschewing controversial subjects connected, with religion, he does not attempt to explain the Egyptian cult of the cat; but he tells us some curious things. For example: if a house is on fire a 'supernatural impulse' inspires the family pets to leap into the flames. The people, standing at a distance, neglect to put out the fire in their anxiety to deter the cats from committing *felo de se*: but these escape by jumping over their heads in order to accomplish their purpose. When all is over there are great lamentations and the bereaved household shaves off its eyebrows in token of mourning. Dead cats are 'taken to certain sacred houses where being first embalmed they are buried in the city of Bubastis'.

Superintendents, both men and women, were appointed to feed every kind of sacred animal, the office being hereditary. When the father of a family had made a vow to some particular beast he proceeded to shave his children's heads, the whole head, or half, or two-thirds. The clippings were then weighed on scales against silver, and whatever the weight might be the silver was handed to the superintendent, who in return 'cut up some fish' and fed it to the object of the vow. This last clause surely applies to the sacred cats only? The sacred crocodile and the sacred ibis would presumably have 'found themselves' in fish.

Some four centuries later Diodorus Siculus was not less impressed by the cult, and he gives us some endearing little glimpses of it in operation. With an amused eye he watched the Egyptians crumbling bread into milk or cutting up fish for the cats, whom they would summon to the banquet 'with a clucking sound'. He notes that anyone who killed an ibis or a cat might be lynched by the populace, with the result that if an Egyptian should catch sight of either animal lying dead he would at once 'withdraw to a great distance and shout with lamentations and protestations' that it was already dead when he found it. Can it have

Cat eating fish under Tawi's chair, wall painting in the Tomb of Nakhts, 1400 BC.

been from Diodorus that Cicero learned that 'no one had ever heard of an Egyptian laying profane hands on a crocodile, an ibis, or a cat'?

This far-travelled historian describes an incident which he himself witnessed when he sojourned in Egypt at the time when Ptolemy Auletes (Ptolemy the Flute-Player) was seeking recognition from the Roman Senate. This Ptolemy was the last of the Hellenistic Kings: with his daughter, Cleopatra, the line of the Ptolemies was extinguished.

At his accession in 80 BC he at once began to angle for the goodwill of Rome. Enormous sums of money changed hands before this grace was won, and protracted negotiations were carried on by Roman envoys whom both the King and the whole of his subjects were extremely anxious to please. By sheer mischance a member of one of these missions happened to kill a cat:

> the multitude rushed to his house, and neither the officials sent by the King to beg the man off nor the fear of Rome (which all the people felt) availed to save him.

Learned gentlemen, both Egyptologists and Zoologists, recognize two types of cat among the surviving cat-mummies: a largish animal perhaps only half-tame and resembling a lynx, living among human habitations but feeding itself; and a smaller form, loosely classed as *felis libyca bubastis*,[2] which became completely domesticated without losing its sacred character.

During the benighted period when human mummy-powder was a popular ingredient in the pharmacopoeia of the West we do not hear of the mummified bodies of cats being used in the same way; but thousands of these were decapitated by Arab husbandmen and then spread upon the fields to act as manure. One-hundred-and-ninety of these lopped-off heads were found at Gizeh and scientifically examined by Mr T. C. S. Morrison-Scott.[3]

On the evidence of the tomb-paintings he attributes to this type of cat long ears (sometimes barred with dark stripes), a ginger-coloured coat, and a long tail with dark rings. MM. Lortet and Gaillard[4] call the colour *gris cendré jauneâtre, mêlés de fauve et de noir*, the tails *annelés de jaune et de noir*: the whiskers, if these survive, are a yellowish white.

The family cat and the temple cat were both punctiliously mummified, but not by so lengthy a process or with such a variety of rare spices as were needed to preserve the mortal remains of their human friends. For kittens, steeping in nitron and banding with linen was often considered adequate, with the result that when such mummies are unwrapped there is to be found only a meagre deposit of dust and a few slender fragments of bone .[5]

More time, money and skill were accorded to fully-grown cats: their wrappings were of two colours, sometimes wound in intricate patterns as if to indicate the characteristic tabby markings. The face is covered by a sort of linen mask with little sprouts representing the ears and eyes, nostrils and whiskers are carefully indicated.

The outer case containing the mummy was fairly substantial and elaborate. A kitten (or even a cat's foetus) might have a little coffin of bronze with the figure of a cat perched on the lid. An adult cat would probably be enclosed in a bronze or wooden receptacle, painted or else sheathed in painted linen, in the shape of a seated *Mau*. One example in the British Museum has a white body surmounted incongruously by a green head. Another has eyes formed of discs of crystal laid upon a gilded surface: the contracted pupils are of black obsidian, the eyelids of bronze. Another, made entirely of bronze, wears an engraved scarab hanging from its collar and an effort has been made to suggest the markings of its fur.

The actual body was as a rule arranged in a sitting posture, the hindquarters flexed, the forepaws lying flat against the flanks, the tail brought up neatly against the belly: but at least one specimen has survived[6] in which the pose is natural and life-like, the cat squatting on its haunches, head up, one paw advanced.

Cat-mummification was practised well into the Roman period.

Curiously enough it was as an aid to agriculture rather than as a divine being that the Romans seem to have prized the animal. Pliny notes that field-mice could be kept away from the crops if the ashes of a cat were soaked in water and then the water itself poured upon the seed. There was, however, one objection to this simple plan; the bread made from the corn was only too apt to 'taste of cat'. It was really better to steep the grain in ox-gall, of which presumably the grain did not taste.

Two Roman writers on agriculture, both flourishing in the first century BC, betray anxiety lest their ducklings should fall a prey to marauding cats. Varro is particularly concerned with the cat-tribe; Columella has also got ferrets on his mind. A fifteen-foot wall, very smoothly plastered, might keep a ferret out of the carefully-planned 'duck-nursery'; but a cat? One is conscious of a little uncertainty on that point.

Mummy of a cat, Roman period after 30 BC, but not in a sitting posture as was common. *British Museum*

Pliny had observed cats closely; the stealth with which their prey is pursued, the daintiness with which it is devoured, their elegant habit of digging a hole when necessary and afterwards scratching the earth over it. Two centuries earlier the independent and freedom-seeking nature of the animal had attracted the notice of those Romans who then raised on the Aventine a statue of the goddess Libertas. In one hand she bore a long rod, in the other one of those Phrygian caps to be notorious in course of time as the Cap of Liberty; at her feet sat a cat. If, as one tradition has it, *Mons Aventinus* was so called because it was the haunt of many birds (*ab avibus*) it was all too appropriate a site for the image of their most unrelenting persecutor. Even the most impassioned cat-lovers of our own softer-hearted days regret this trait. In modern eyes it was a cruel whim which prompted the owner of the Casa del Fauno at Pompeii to choose a mosaic design showing a particularly ferocious though certainly decorative tabby with a despairing domestic fowl held captive in his claws.

The fables attributed to Æsop were widely current in the Roman Empire at this time, and it may be that one of them inspired the Pompeian mosaic.

The Cat, having a Mind to make a Meal of the Cock, seized him one Morning by surprise and asked him what he could say for himself why Slaughter should not pass upon him. The Cock replied that he was serviceable to Mankind by crowing in the Morning and calling them to their daily Labour.

'That is true,' says the Cat, 'and is the very objection that I have against you; for you make such a shrill, impertinent Noise that People cannot sleep for you. Besides, you are an incestuous Rascal who make no Scruple of lying with your Mother and Sisters.' 'Well,' says the Cock, 'This I do not deny, but I do it to procure Eggs and Chickens for my Master.' 'Ah, Villain,' says the Cat. 'Hold your wicked Tongue. Such Impieties as these declare that you are no longer fit to live.'[7]

The Cat and the Cock from *Æsop's Fables*, after Francis Clein.

Another fable[8] tells of a house much infested with mice, and of the successful efforts of an active cat to keep their numbers down. The mice in council resolved that none of them should descend from the topmost shelf. Then the cat,

> hungry and disappointed of her Prey, had recourse to this Stratagem. She hung by her hinder Legs on a Peg which stuck in the Wall and made as if she had been dead, hoping by this lure to entice the Mice to come down. She had not been in this Posture long before a cunning old Mouse peeped over the Edge of the Shelf and spoke thus: 'Aha, my good Friend, are you there? There may you be! I would not trust myself with You though your Skin were stuffed with Straw.'

A third fable records a conversation between a Fox and a cat, Reynard offering to teach her 'a Number of Tricks in case of Need' and she confessing that she knew but one: 'and if that won't do, I am undone'. Immediately after 'a Pack of Hounds came upon them in full Cry'. Poor Reynard for all his numerous tricks was slain, but the Cat, having recourse to her only one, escaped all danger. She ran up a tree.

The fable of the cat transformed into a woman appeared and reappeared through the centuries, in Greek, in Latin, and finally in French. In the following version the background is obviously classical; one hears the swish of the Roman toga on the tessellated pavement of a Roman villa.

The frustrated cat *Æsop's Fables*, after a 1479 woodcut.

The Cat and
the Fox from
*Æsop's Fables*,
after Francis
Clein.

A cat was seized with love for a certain handsome young man, and
prayed Venus to change her into a woman. The goddess had pity
on her and transformed her to a pretty girl, and the young man was
struck by her singular beauty and took her to his house. They were
sitting together on a couch when Venus, wishing to see if the lady had
changed her habits with the change in her person, suddenly sent down
a mouse between them. The cat, forgetful of her present state, rose
from the couch and started in pursuit of the mouse from a passionate
longing to devour it, and the goddess in anger turned her back to her
original shape.

The fable shows that men are by nature miserable sinners who may
change their rank and station, but never change their manners to
correspond.

When La Fontaine retells the ancient story we at once find ourselves in the Paris of Louis XIV. No pagan god or goddess is invoked by name, nor does any supernatural influence intervene when the deed has been done. And this time it is the youth who becomes enamoured of a cat, a beautiful, affectionate and elegant cat.

Nothing is said about Venus. It is *le destin* who pities his tears, heeds his prayers, and works the miracle by changing the creature into a woman. The suppliant at once decides to make her his wife. Never was there a more charming bride nor a more devoted bridegroom. Her real nature is completely forgotten. Then by ill hap they are disturbed by a mouse gnawing at the matting. Up starts the bride, ready to pounce upon the intruder. She misses the first time, but crouches for a second spring. The mouse, deceived by her New Look, ventures forth again: but this time she does not miss.

Here the *talon-rouge* version of the story is brought to a close, except for some platitudes on the force of Nature and the overworked old tag from the Tenth Epistle of Horace's First Book:

*Naturam expelles furca tamen usque recurret.*

(You may drive nature out with a pitchfork but somehow she will come back.)

*Le destin* does not seem to have taken any further interest in the mouse-hunting lady: we do not hear of her being restored to her original form, and we are left to imagine what were the feelings of her lord if the disconcerting interlude were enacted a second time.

# Some Celtic and Medieval Cats

It cannot be said that either the Greeks or the Romans were interested in cats. Even in the ancient fable of the Town Mouse and the Country Mouse it was, according to Horace, a watch-dog and not a cat which broke up the banquet of the two nibbling sisters. On the other hand, the Celtic peoples of the West, especially the Irish and the Cymry, gave the cat a place not only in their legends but in their legal codes.

The animal whom they thus honoured seems to have been brought—with many other things of rarity and beauty from the East. She was not a tamed Wild Cat; she was a descendant—if only collateral—of *felis libyca bubastis*. At first she may have been regarded as a pet, like the apes and peacocks imported from the land of Punt by Queen Hatshepsut; but her prowess as a mouse-slayer soon commended her to her masters from a more utilitarian point of view, and a tenth-century Welsh King, Howell Dha the Good, included the following law in his famous code:

> The price of a kitten before it can see is one penny. If it has caught a mouse, its value is raised to twopence, and afterwards to fourpence. If anyone should steal or slay the cat guarding the royal granary, he shall be compelled either to forfeit an ewe or as much wheat as will cover the cat when suspended by its tail.

The story of the Voyage of Maelduin as retold in Lady Gregory's *Book of Saints and Wonders* introduces a cat which is both life-like and eerie.

Maelduin, the adopted son of an Irish Queen, sets out to avenge the death of his actual father, who had been slain by robbers 'and his church burned over him'. With his three foster-brothers he fared forth in a curragh-boat of his own fashioning 'having three skins on it' and after incredible adventures they sighted a small island on which stood a lofty dun or stronghold with walls as white as if they were 'all one rock of chalk'. The dun was wide open, and round it stood many new houses of the same colour, also deserted and unbarred. Maelduin and his brothers went into the best of these houses, and found there no living thing but a little cat, 'playing about on the four stone pillars that were there and leaping from one to the other'. Apparently these pillars were considerably lower than the roof, or else had capitals with ledges wide enough to accommodate a cat. She looked at the strangers for a short space, but did not pause in her play.

They then noticed that round the wall of the house, reaching from one door-post to the other, were three rows of dazzling treasure; the first was a row of brooches of gold and silver; the second was a row of collars of gold and silver; and the third was a row of great swords having hilts of gold and silver. Moreover, in the authentic fairy-tale tradition, refreshments were waiting; a roasted ox on a fire in the middle of the house, and large vessels with good fermented liquor.

'Is it for us that all this is left here?' asked Maelduin of the cat.

She looked at him for a minute and then returned to her play.

Reassured, they ate and drank, and laid themselves down to sleep. When they woke they thriftily gathered up all that remained of the repast; and just as they were making ready to depart the third brother was struck by an unlucky idea that he might possibly bear one of the rich collars away with him. 'Do not,' said Maelduin, 'for it is not without a guard that this house is.'

In spite of this warning the young man took one of the necklaces and carried it as far as the centre of the dun.

And the cat came after him and leaped through him like a fiery arrow, and burned him till he was but ashes, and it made a leap back again on to its pillar.

Maelduin handled the situation with admirable presence of mind. He spoke soothing words to the cat, put the necklace back in its place, cleared away the ashes of the victim and flung them on the shore of the sea.

And they went back into the curragh praising and making much of the Lord.

These Celtic chroniclers seem to have been conscious of the slightly mysterious and sometimes sinister atmosphere clinging round the cat.[1] This element is even more conspicuous in the story of St Brendan and the Sea Cat, as retold by Helen Waddell in that enchanting book, *Beasts and Saints*.

This Saint in the course of his journeyings came to a lovely little island flanked by a strange whirlpool in which, when the tide receded, great multitudes of fishes could be caught. He and his companions landed, and found a small stone-built church wherein was a very frail and aged man kneeling at his prayers. His first words were to urge them to flee from the place; 'for', said he, 'there is a sea-cat here of old time, inveterate in wiles, that hath grown huge through eating excessively of fish'.

St Brendan and his little company hastily set sail again, and presently saw swimming after them a beast with 'great eyes like vessels of glass'. The Saint at once implored the Lord Jesus Christ to 'hinder the beast'. Then another beast rose from the sea, and the two fought fiercely with each other, and at last both went down into the depths and were seen no more.

Giving thanks to God they landed again and sought out the old man, and questioned him. He said:

> We were twelve men from the island of Ireland that came to this place seeking the place of our resurrection. Eleven be dead, and I alone remain, awaiting, O Saint of God, the Host from thy hands. We brought with us in the ship a cat, a most amiable cat and greatly loved by us; but he grew to great bulk through eating of fish, as I said: yet our Lord Jesus Christ did not suffer him to harm us.

And when, having received the Host from St Brendan's hands, the old man 'fell joyfully asleep in the Lord', he was buried beside his companions on the island.

In these Irish annals we also read of four scholars who went to sea 'for the love of God', taking nothing with them; but the youngest of the four had an afterthought. 'I think', he said, 'I will take the little cat.'

Another Irish cat was Pangur Bán,[2] the property of a learned monk who wrote a charming poem upon him. When the two of them are alone together, the black-habited monk and the comely white cat, each has something upon which to exercise his wit. One pursues a mouse, the other pursues a difficult saying, hard to understand, in his 'little book'.

*Above and below:* Illustrations of Pangur Ban from medieval manuscripts.

The association between the cat and the religious life continued long after the heathen in his blindness had been wont to bow down to cats of wood and stone. The wise and kindly ecclesiastic who drew up in the thirteenth century the *Ancren Riwle* (or anchoress's code) for the guidance of a small Cistercian community of recluses understood human nature too well to try the flesh too high or to cut off every outlet of affection. Though inculcating the strictest asceticism, he does not wish his 'dear sisters' to wear hair-shirts, walk barefoot, beat themselves with holly and briars or subsist on pulse and water. Milk is allowed in their dietary, and the anchoress was even allowed a cat, with whom one is sure that she shared the contents of her bowl. 'Ye, mine leove sustren,' says the Rule, 'ne schulen haben no Best bute Kat one' (Ye, my dear sisters, shall have no beast but one cat).

Perhaps 'kat one' was needed to keep the recluse's cell free from rats and mice; but it would be a companion as well, and during the long hours when its mistress was alone, neither exchanging a few permitted remarks through the grating with some carefully-chosen acquaintance nor in grave converse with her confessor, it seems impossible that she did not talk to her pet, or utter loving words as the arched back rubbed against her grey-clad knee, the faithful head bumped up into her down-stretched hand, or the deep purr gave a momentary illusion of an articulate answer.

No visiting Bishop however stern seems ever to have deprecated the keeping of cats in cloisters. Small dogs, monkeys, even tame rabbits, might disturb the community, distract their minds, befoul their paved walks; but a cat could be trusted to behave with decorum. If she (or he) strayed from the narrow path marked out for the nuns, the straying was effected unobtrusively, and no scandal followed.

The nuns at Carrow, in Northumberland, certainly had a cat in the early years of the sixteenth century, a 'Gib cat'[3] who pounced upon and slew Jane Scrope's pet sparrow, as related in John Skelton's lament for that ill-fated bird. 'Gibbe our catte' was merely obeying the instincts of his kind, but the bereaved Jane would fain have meted out to him some exemplary punishment.

Cat's fur is frequently mentioned in those complicated sumptuary laws which were so much easier to lay down than to enforce, especially when they ran counter to the wilfulness of womankind. At one time a woman's dress was regulated by her husband's income, not in relation to what he could afford but according to what their social status made it seem suitable that she should wear. Miniver and marten, gryse and vair were the prerogative of royal and noble persons, but the mild lamb, humble cat and the still more lowly rabbit-skin were the portion of those of lower degree. Cat's fur was for some reason regarded as particularly suitable to be worn by nuns; but one cannot imagine even the sternest Lady Abbess giving orders that some deceased pet of the convent should contribute its hide to line her winter slippers.

Bartholomew the Englishman, writing of the cat in his encyclopaedic work, *De Natura Rerum*, has many things to say that are as true today,

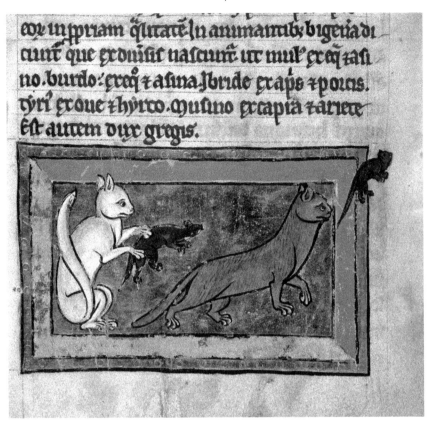

A medieval manuscript depicting cats mousing. *British Library*

A medieval Jewish manuscript depicting cats under the table.

and will be as true tomorrow, as they were in the thirteenth century when he wrote, and in the fourteenth when John Trevisa translated him.

The cat is in youth, he tells us, 'a full lecherous beast'. He is swift, pliant and merry, he leapeth and climbeth on everything that is before him; he is led by a straw and playeth therewith,

> and is a right heavy beast in age, and full sleepy, and lieth slyly in wait for mice, and is aware where they be more by smell than by sight, and hunteth and pounceth upon them in privy places. And when he taketh a mouse he playeth therewith and eateth him after the play.

There is sometimes 'hard fighting for wives': the wooers scratch each other grievously with teeth and claws. They make a 'ruthful noise and ghastful when one proffereth to fight with another'; they can be thrown down from high places and not be hurt.

> And when he hath a fair skin he is as it were proud thereof and goeth fast about: but when his skin is burnt,[4] then he abideth at home. And is oft for his fair skin taken by the skinner, and slain and flayed.

Bartholomew was a Friar Minor, a follower of that first and greatest of animal-lovers, St Francis. The Franciscans did not live in cloisters: they were wandering and preaching Friars; but they had their Houses, where they might sojourn between their missionary journeys, and where they might meet for study or consultation; and some of them, Roger Bacon and Bartholomew the Englishmen among them, lectured, and so, presumably, for a time resided in Universities such as those of Paris and Oxford. The encyclopaedist must have been familiar with the academic and ecclesiastical cat, kept to guard the meagrely-stocked larders of the order, and to ward off the mice and rats which might otherwise have invaded their austere habitations.

Though the Latin for a cat is the feminine noun *felis*, and though the English habit of alluding to cats and ships (and later engines) as 'she' extends through many centuries, Trevisa, himself an ecclesiastic, firmly makes Brother Bartholomew's animal a male cat. Was a male more in favour as an auxiliary in colleges and conventional buildings? Were the brethren willing to endure the 'ruthful noise and ghastful' of his amorous ditties rather than find themselves overrun with constantly recurring families of lively kittens?

Detail of a bas-de-page scene of a donkey playing a trumpet and a cat beating a tabor. England, between 1310 and 1320. *British Library*

It is not difficult to imagine Brother Bartholomew watching a merry young cat leaping and pouncing. Perhaps he rose from his knees sometimes, extracted a long; tempting straw from the strewing of his cell, and indulged in a quiet frolic with the swift and pliant creature. He knew its tricks of torturing and beguiling the wretched mouse before eating it:[5] perhaps it was he himself who, when the 'ruthful noise' became an intolerable hindrance to meditation and prayer, threw down the delinquent from a high place, only to perceive (one hopes with some measure of relief) that he was little the worse.

That same cat may have lived to be the 'right heavy beast and full sleepy' whom Friar Bartholomew remembered well. Friars wore no fur, not even catskin, on their humble habits, but it was otherwise with monks and nuns of less austere orders. The 'fair skin' of a Franciscan cat may have trimmed the sleeve of a Benedictine Abbot, thus perpetuating the association between poor puss and the religious world.

Cats and dogs must certainly have learned to tolerate each other's society in those medieval households which provided snug if stuffy and smoky harbourage for them both. 'To drive out the cat and the dog' is specifically mentioned as one of the duties of the gentleman-usher preparing a royal prince's bedchamber in the fifteenth century. Was either of these animals ever permitted to spend a night on the too-tempting royal bed when the long curtains looped up at each end of the four corners were let down and drawn forward? If either of them succeeded in doing so one hazards a guess that it was the cat. Like the Puss in Æsop's fable, she could always exercise her one trick and jump or climb whether upon a bed or up a tree. An opening was often made in the bottom of the bedroom door for her convenience. Why a small dog should not have gone in and out in the same way is not clear; but it is always the cat who is mentioned in this connection. In the Miller's Tale we see Robyn, the young serving-man of the Oxford Carpenter, stooping and peering through a hole

> ful low upon a bord
> Ther as the cat was wont in for to crepe.

As the door was that of Hendy Nicholas's chamber he or should we say Chaucer?—felt no uneasiness lest the intruder should pluck at the strings of his 'gay sautrie', knock over his astrolabe, make havoc among his 'bokés grete and smale', or set his augrim-stones rolling over the floor.

In order to 'sleep soft' it was not always necessary for a Plantagenet cat to creep through a hole in his master's door or to invade his bed. We are reminded of the fables of the metamorphosed cat when we recall this well-known passage in the Manciple's Tale.

> Lat take a cat and fostre hym wel with milk[6]
> And tendré flessch and make his couche of silk,
> And lat hym seen a mous go by the wal,
> Anon he weyvith milk and flessh and al,
> And every deyntee that is in that hous,
> Swich appetit he hath to ete a mous.

The Wyf of Bath had also observed the habits of the cat kind, though she is more interested in the she-cat than the male. A well-read woman both in sacred and profane literature, she can confute a captious husband by quoting the *Almagest* of 'Daun Ptholome', and she can flout his reminder of the awkward text in I Timothy, chapter ii, verse 9, concerning modest apparel by citing a homely, familiar example:

> —if the cattés skyn by slyk and gay
> She wol nat dwelle in house half a day
> But forth she wole, er any day be dawed,
> To shewe her skyn and goon-a-caterwawed.[7]

A woodcut from the prologue to *Canterbury Tales* by Geoffrey Chaucer.

A fable which came home forcibly to the English people during the troubled reign of Richard II was the fable of the mice (or rats) who wanted to hang a bell round the neck of their arch-enemy, the Cat. It was retold by William Langland,[8] but the Cat is clearly the symbol of the oppressive and extortionate ruling class which the King, being still only a 'kitten', was powerless to control.

Here we see the rats in conclave speaking bitterly of 'a Cat of a courte' who goes where he will, plays with them perilously, pushes them about. They are full of fears. If they were to rebel against his game, he would bring grief upon them all,

> Scratch us, or claw us, or in his clutches hold.
> Might we with any wit his will withstand
> We might be lords aloft and live at our ease.

A 'rat of renown' then remarks that in London he has seen knights and squires wandering at their will with bright collars round their necks.

Now if there were but bells upon those collars! 'Reason me showeth,' says the rat, 'to make a bell of brass or bright silver, and knit it upon a collar and hang it upon the Cat's neck.' Then they might know whether he was roaming or slumbering or running to play.

The rats agreed with enthusiasm, bought a bell, and fixed it to a collar. But

> There was no rat of all the rout
> That durst have bound the bell about the Cat's neck.

A wise mouse then stood forth and reminded the disappointed rats that even if the Cat were slain yet there would come another to scratch them and all their kind, even though they 'crept under benches'. His advice is to let the cat be, and never be so bold as to show him the bell. Suffer and say nought. It is the safest way in the end.

It was not thus that a secret meeting of malcontent Scottish barons rounded off the fable in the reign of that misfit among monarchs, the artistic, fantastic James III. Malcontent Barons seem to have preferred churches as plotting-places: one remembers the Magna Charta rebels in the Abbey of St Edmund Bury. It was in the church at Lauder that the Scots assembled to discuss the evils brought upon the land by the King, with special reference to his favourite, the architect Cochran. Lord Gray reminded them of the story:

> which was as much as to intimate that though the discontented nobles might make bold resolutions against the King's ministers yet it would be difficult to find anyone courageous enough to act upon them. Archibald Douglas, Earl of Angus, a man of gigantic strength and intrepid courage, ... started up when Gray had done speaking: 'I am he', he said, 'who will bell the cat!' From which expression he was distinguished by the name of 'Bell the Cat' till his dying day.[9]

In the event it was a halter not a bell which was tied round the wretched Cochran's neck: nor can it be said that Archibald Douglas brought about this deed unaided. The anecdote is relevant as showing how strong a hold cat-and-mouse fables took upon the minds of men of action at a time when the Scottish Barons are believed to have been a relatively uncouth and unlettered gang.

Though the fifteenth-century Scottish dominie, Robert Henryson, borrowed from the fable called Æsop's the story of the Town (or Burges) and the Country (or Uplandis) Mouse, he invests it with a curious Scottish charm.

It is over Scottish moors and mountains, through 'brown heath and shaggy wood', that the Burges Mouse wends her arduous way to visit her 'rycht solitar' sister, by whom she is most affectionately received. A repast of nuts and dried peas is set before the distinguished stranger, but it is disdainfully rejected. Neither the teeth nor the 'wame'[10] of the Burges Mouse will tolerate this 'rude dyet'. Let her Uplandis sister come to town, and taste her *daily* fare.

Great indeed is the contrast between those rough and harsh foods and the banquet spread to regale the astonished country guest; cheese and butter, flesh and fish, malt and meal. But presently the Spencer or Butler arrives, keys in hand. The Burges Mouse bolts into her hole; her Uplandis sister flattens herself quivering upon the floor. The Spencer departs. The little creatures creep out again. And now another, greater danger looms up: the family cat.

> —in come Gib Hunter, our jolly cat,
> And bade 'God speed'. The Burges up with that
> And to the hole she went as fire from flint.
> Bawdrons[11] the other by the back has hint.[12]
> From foot to foot he cast her to and fro,
> Whiles up, whiles down, as cant[13] as any kid;
> Whiles would he let her run under the straw
> Whiles would he wink and play with her butshid;[14]
> Thus to the silly Mouse great pain he did,
> While at the last through fortune and good hap
> Betwixt ane boardé and the wall she crap.

The Uplandis Mouse expresses herself with some energy when the peril is past.

> Thy mangerie is mingled all with care,
> Thy goose is good, thy sauce is sour as gall;
> I thank you curtain and you perpall[15] wall
> Of my defence now from a cruel Beast.

Henryson, having set the Uplandis Mouse safely on her way back to the wild heath, offers the *Moralitas* of the fable.

> O wanton man, that uses for to feed
>    Thy wame[16] and makest it a god to be,

Look to thyself I warn thee well, but[17] dread
The Cat cometh and to the Mouse has e'e.

In the fifteenth century the usefulness of a cat as a protector of homes and crops against mice was recognized in the codes and customs of various European countries. When Louis XI was out hunting with harriers at Montlouis, between Tours and Amboise, his hounds fell upon and killed the cat of a poor cottage woman. Though not the most open-handed of monarchs, he gave the good dame a crown—the same sum that would have been indicated if the victim had been a goose or a sheep.

A medieval manuscript domestic scene with a cat in the background.

The heralds of medieval England preferred dogs to cats as crests and supporters in coats of arms. Their *confrères* north of the Border seem to have been more interested in the wild than in the domestic beast from a professional point of view. The cat *sejeant gardant proper* of the Grants of Ballindalloch is no 'Jolly Gib' but a real cat-a-mountain; hence, no doubt, the warning motto, *Touch not the cat but*[18] *a glove*; the Macintosh clan of Caithness, the descendants of the Catti or Clan Chattan, bore the same motto, and had two cats *salient gardant proper* as their supporters. The ducal house of Sutherland also bears a cat-a-mountain *salient*. The present Duke tells us[19] that there is a tradition that the family owes its descent through the female line from some doughty Northern invader who, on landing at Littleferry, about four miles from Dunrobin, was pounced upon by a number of ferocious wild cats. The fight that ensued was fierce and long, but in the end all the cats were slain, and the courageous invader became the first Thane of Sutherland.

The most celebrated cat in heraldry was probably one which existed only in the jangling imagination of Don Quixote de la Mancha. Among the knights whom he believed that he beheld when he came upon a peacefully-grazing flock of sheep was a certain Timonel de Carcajona, Prince of New Biscay, whose shield bore the figure of a cat, and the laconic motto, *Miau*.

Artists, like heralds, preferred dogs to cats. Hound or lapdog, shaggy or sleek, the dogs pervade the painted world, while cats characteristically hold themselves aloof. Pinturicchio did, however, introduce an uncommonly pleasing tabby into his picture of the Return of Ulysses.

Penelope sits at her loom in the Palace of Ithaca. One of her balls of wool has dropped on the floor, and her cat, it seems hardly more than a kitten, is sporting with it, demurely rather than friskily, regardless of the foppish wooer who advances hawk on wrist and of the bearded stranger, presumably the King himself, entering in a purposeful manner by a distant door.

Tintoretto's dusky, couchant cat in the picture of Christ washing the Disciple's Feet is another aloof specimen, so dark in colour, so withdrawn in pose, that only quick eyes can detect her presence.

Among the liveliest of the medieval English miracle-plays was that of the Deluge, acted by the Waterdrawers of Chester. As the animals (represented by what would now be called 'cut-outs') were hustled aboard the Ark, Noah's three sons, with some assistance from their wives, call out their names. There is a rather ominous conjunction in Japhet's

take here cattés and doggés too:

and the audience, always on the alert for a jest, could be trusted to perceive that this arrangement did not promise well for a peaceful voyage. But there was worse to come. Shem's wife adds:

> Yet more beastés are in this house:
> Here cattés maken it full crowse;
> Here a ratton, there a mouse,
> They stand nye together.

In the fifteenth-century English as in some modern Scottish dialects 'crowse' means cheerful or lively; but in earlier usage the word could carry another significance, namely wrathful. What was in Mrs Shem's mind? Were the 'cattés' in a gay or in a fierce humour when they found themselves 'nye' their wonted victims? Perhaps the answer should be 'both'.

The legend of the cat who by ridding an Oriental potentate's palace of rats and mice won a fortune for her lucky owner pervades the folklore of Europe. It is ancient, it is pleasant, it is immortal. How it became attached to the honoured name of Richard Whittington it is impossible to tell. Certainly it was not anywhere near the life-time of the Flower of Merchants. 'The famous fable of Whittington and his Puss' is mentioned in *Eastward Hoe!*[20] (1605): so it was then already famous, and already

Black cats Bestiary, England thirteenth century. *Bodleian Library, MS. Bodl. 533*

recognized as a fable. Many Londoners were, however, inclined to question its fabulous character. Outward from the capital it grew. Pedlars hawked it about the country in uncouth prose and even more uncouth verse. Nurses retold it to listening children round the fire. Pepys saw it represented in a puppet-show at Southwark Fair, and found it 'pretty to see'. And then, reaching the final stage of its long journey, the story invaded the stage of the Christmas pantomime, where the great mercer-mayor was 'translated', even more strangely than Bully Bottom was, from a grave City worthy into a smiling and warbling woman, while his cat gambolled and mewed in the form of a man.

Some pedants have tried to trace the tale to an 'achat' or Bill of Exchange: others have prated of a type of medieval merchant-vessel called a 'catt'; but popular imagination was loth to let the cat go, the actual tabby who journeyed to the land of Barbary and there wrought a sad havoc among the vermin infesting the palace of the King. There was joy among the true believers when in 1862 some workmen digging near the site of a house in Gloucester traditionally associated with the Whittington family unearthed a small carving of a boy holding something that looked uncommonly like a cat: but, after their fashion, the doubters continued to doubt.

An old picture of the Tudor period showing a man in liveryman's costume with his hand on a skull was wildly identified as a portrait of Whittington. An enterprising engraver got to work upon it, and by changing the skull into a cat produced a print which brought him rich returns.

Abortive efforts were made not long since to discover the grave of Whittington beneath the bomb-battered ruins of St Michael's Paternoster Royal. The church wrecked by the Luftwaffe was a Wren, and not the fifteenth-century edifice restored and enriched by the best remembered of London worthies, who had been disturbed in his last sleep long before the Blitz crashed over his City. Lured by a legend of gold and treasure buried in the coffin a caitiff Reformed parson of Edward VI's bleak reign broke it open. In the following reign the parishioners reopened the vault and enfolded the desecrated relics in lead. It could hardly have been expected that two Great Fires would leave unscathed so perishable an integument: but what the explorers *did* find in the course of their search was the wizened body of a cat. Alas, she could not possibly have been coeval with Richard Whittington: nor is any *felis* (nor, indeed, any *navis*) mentioned in the Latin epitaph that has survived the rich sepulchre upon which it was piously engraved five hundred years ago.

A later engraving of
Richard Whittington.

But the legend lives. A poet of our own time[21] has retold it through
the lips of Gregory Clopton, Clerk of the Bell of Bow. Master Gregory
would have given the lie to any Londoner who spoke of 'fables' in that
connection. He tells of Whittington as the little scullion he never was,
sleeping in the rat-haunted attic where probably he never slept, and
spending his 'first poor penny piece' to buy a cat, which he may very
well have bought, if he was a cat-lover and a rat-hater. He shows us
the boy abashed because of Fitz-Warren's household he alone has no
single coin to stake upon his master's trading venture in the good ship
*Unicorn*, and then staking his cat. How could the Clerk of the Bell of
Bow relate the story otherwise? The final picture is so lovely that even
pedants and sceptics will wish it were true: or perhaps hope that it may
be true after all.

> So when the painted ship
> Sailed through a golden sunrise down the Thames
> A grey tail waved upon the misty poop
> And Whittington had his venture out at sea.

# Tudor and Shakespearean Cats

We meet A Tudor cat in the 'ryght pithy, plesaunt and merie Comedie intytled *Gammer Gurton's Needle*' played for the first time by scholars of Christ's College, Cambridge, in the first year of Edward VI's brief reign. It is, indeed, owing to 'Gyb' that the precious needle, the 'fayre, longe, strayght neele' is lost, good neighbours come to blows, a false alarm of fire is raised—always a terrifying thought to dwellers in those huddled, highly-inflammable timber tenements—and the parson and the bailie have to be summoned to cope with the general uproar.

Gammer Gurton's serving-man Hodge is anxious to be able to go to church on a certain Sunday, not from any devout inclination but because 'Kirstian Clack, Tom Simson's maid' had smiled at him the week before when he 'put off his cap'. Then he found with concern that there was a prodigious rent in the rear of his breeches, and his mistress sat herself down to clap a patch over the hole.

A bowl of milk intended for Hodge's dinner stood on the board: and then, as she glanced up from her sewing, Gammer Gurton spied 'Gyb our cat' over head and ears in the milk. '"Out, thief," she cried aloud, and cast the breeches down: up went her staff and out leapt Gyb at doors into the town.' This was prudent on the part of Gyb, for the Gammer lost her needle when she 'cast the breeches down', and the extravagance of her distress is better understood when we remember that a needle was a rare and costly object in the sixteenth century. Although the Needlemakers' Company had been granted a charter by Henry VIII, Gammer Gurton's precious implement was the work of a spurrier. 'Implement' seems the correct term, all things considered: if the mending of leather garments was one of the purposes for which it was needed a small steel object such as those imported from Damascus to Nuremberg in the fourteenth century would have been quite inadequate. So the Gammer has lost her needle and Hodge has lost his dinner, and Gyb has fled.

A great hunt is instituted. Tyb the maid sifts all the household dust through her fingers and Hodge rakes the dead ashes of the fire, while the Gammer never ceases to bewail her treasure.

In the meantime Gyb has crept back again, only to cause further dismay and alarm. Though the ashes are dead-cold Hodge imagines that he sees two sparks glowing in the shadow. The sequel is related by Cocke, the servant-lad. Those sparks

> —were indeed nought else but Gyb our cat's two eyes.
> 'Puff!' quoth Hodge, thinking thereby to have fire without doubt:
> With that Gyb shut her two eyes and so the fire was out,
> And by and bye them opened, even as they were before.
> With that the sparks appeared even as they had done of yore.
> And even as Hodge blew the fire, as he did think,
> Gyb as she felt the blast straightway began to wink,
> Till Hodge fell to swearing, as came best to his turn,
> The fire was sure bewitched and therefore would not burn.

The affronted Gyb then flees upstairs to the attic, and Hodge, fearing that the supposed sparks will set the thatch on fire, stumbles after her and barks his shins. 'Come down, Hodge,' commands Gammer Gurton, 'and let the cat alone.' She tells him that it is the cat's eyes which he has seen shining, and when he seems sceptical she declares that 'they shine as like fire as ever man did see'.

Gyb's troubles are not yet over. Diccon, the half-crazy Bedlam beggar, steals a morsel of bacon which Hodge has had his eye upon, and Gyb naturally is blamed. And then the suggestion is made that the missing 'neele' may be in the cat's maw. She is observed to be gasping as if in some discomfort, and her mistress, now taking a gloomy view of everything, exclaims 'Farewell, Gyb, thou art undone and lost!' Yet even in that moment of despair she remembers that Gyb dead may be worth more than Gyb living, for she adds, lost—all save the skin'. Hodge is anxious to seize his knife and slit open the poor beast's throat, but the Gammer will not hear of it. What! Nay, Hodge, fie! Kill not our cat. 'Tis all the cats we have now.'

With several lives still in hand, Gyb was well able to escape this third danger. She appears for the last time just before the discovery of the

needle accidentally embedded in Hodge's rear-quarters brings the farce
to an uproarious close.

When the bailie imposes an oath upon the neighbour who had come to
blows with Gammer Gurton he binds her likewise to be 'of good bearing to
Gyb her great cat': from which it appears that feuds between neighbours
sometimes involved their pets, as such feuds are apt to do to this day.

Some twenty years after the first production of *Gammer Gurton's Needle*
there appeared the earliest English book upon Natural History, *A Greene
Forest* by John Maplet. He borrows freely from our old friend Bartholomew
Anglicus, but in dealing with the cat he shows some originality and draws
upon other sources of information—or misinformation.

> The Cat in Latin is called *Catus*,[1] as if you would say *Cautus*, wary or
> wise . . . She is to the Mouse a Continuall Enemie: verie like to the Lyon
> in toothe and clawe, and useth in pastime to play with the Mouse ere she
> devourith him. She is in her trade and maner of living very shame-fast,
> always loving clenlinesse. There is also a kind hereof called the Wild
> Cat, which of all things is annoyed with the smell of Rue and of Almond
> leaf, and is driven away with that sooner than with any other thing.

Edward Topsell followed on with his famous and fantastic Bestiary,
the *Book of Beasts* (1607). It is interesting to compare his remarks on

Edward Topsell's woodcut of a cat from his
History of Four-footed Beasts.

the Cat with John Maplet's quoted above and with those set down three centuries earlier by Brother Bartholomew. The Friar may have watched the cat of some community, his devotions may have been broken by his ghastly and ruthful voice: but Topsell must have had a cat of his own. 'It is needless', he says,

> to spend any time about her loving nature to man; how she flattereth by rubbing her skinne against one's legges, how she whurleth with her voice, having as many tones as tunes; for she hath one voice to beg and to complain, another to testifie her delight and pleasure, another among her own kind by flattring, by hissing, by spitting, in so much that some have thought they had a particular intelligible language among themselves.

Fitting Shakespeare's words into an imaginary framework of his own thoughts and feelings is a perilous pastime in which all too many people have indulged ere now. Yet it seems not impossible to guess something of what he felt towards the family cat at New Place and the cat-tribe in general if we follow poor Puss from play to play. Let us face the unwelcome conclusion. He loved cats even less than he did dogs, and that was not much.

Had he an allergy? If not, he must have been well acquainted with someone who 'went mad' if he beheld 'the harmless, necessary cat'. Those two epithets, 'harmless' and 'necessary', are the only two tolerant, much less kindly words he can find to attach to the animal. The same heart that could feel a pang for 'poor Wat', the hunted hare, far off upon a hill, standing 'on hinder leg with listening ear', for the galled pack-horse, the overspurred nag, the gallant charger fallen in the field, the captive birds quivering on the limed twigs, the hound 'embossed' with sweat after a hard run, had no pity for the cat wedged in a leather bottle and shot at with arrows for the amusement of the mob.

The suggestion of an allergy occurs again in *All's Well*. Bertram suffered from one. He shows it when he expresses his rising aversion to Parolles: 'I could endure anything before but a cat and now he's a cat to me'; 'more and more a cat'; 'a pox on him, he's a cat still'. Thersites in *Troilus and Cressida* lumps together 'a dog, a mule, a cat, a fitchew, a toad, a lizard, an owl, a puttock'. The fitchew was a polecat: it is curious to see Shakespeare associating it in his mind with the domestic cat as the Greeks of the later pre-Christian period had been wont to do.

*A Book of Cats*

That least amiable of women, the Queen in *Cymbeline*, discussing with Dr Cornelius her desire to experiment with deadly poisons, seeks to reassure him by a promise that she will try the forces of his compounds on such creatures as were 'counted not worth the hanging'. By this he took her to mean cats and dogs: and there is a welcome gleam of compunction in his warning to her that she would 'from this practice but make hard her heart'.

There are only two cat-allusions in the Roman plays, both in *Coriolanus*. Marcius, telling Cominius how the besieged Volscians had beaten the Romans back to their trenches, remarks angrily that 'the mouse ne'er shunned the cat as they did budge from rascals worse than they'; and Volumnia, heaping reproaches on Brutus after the banishment of her son, tells him that it was he who incensed the rabble,

> Cats, that can judge as fitly of his worth
> As I can of those mysteries which heaven
> Will not have earth to know.

The choice of metaphor is curious. Cats do not form themselves into packs to harry their enemies. Wolves, or even hounds, would have seemed a more intelligible analogy. Again we find in Shakespeare traces of an aversion which may have amounted to an allergy.

Mercutio, when deriding Tybalt in conversation with Benvolio, calls him a 'prince of cats': when he forces a duel upon this 'lisping, affecting fantastico', this 'rat-catcher' and Tybalt asks him, 'What wouldst thou have with me?' he answers, 'Good king of cats, nothing but one of your nine lives': and when, owing to Romeo's ill-timed though well-meant intervention, Tybalt gives him what—with the cat-image still in his mind—he calls 'a scratch, a scratch', almost his last thought finds utterance in the bitter cry, 'Zounds, a dog, a rat, a mouse, a cat, to scratch a man to death!' Romeo loved cats no better than Mercutio did, or the Queen in *Cymbeline*. Many mice must have haunted the rush-strewn floors of Renaissance houses, and not a few cats must have been needed to keep them down.

Hence the banished lover's cry to Friar Lawrence:

> —heaven is here
> Where Juliet lives; and every cat and dog
> And little mouse, every unworthy thing,
> Lives here in heaven and may look on her.

It would appear that Shakespeare's immortals also thought poorly of the cat, and ranked her as an 'unworthy thing'. When Oberon mentions the various unlikeable animals whom Titania might conceivably take for her true love on awakening from enchanted slumber, he says

> Be it mouse, or cat, or bear,
> Pard or boar with bristled hair.

There are few cat-allusions in. the Histories. Falstaff proclaims himself 'as melancholy as a Gib cat or a lugged bear'; Westmorland speaks of the 'weasel Scot' playing the mouse in absence of the cat and making havoc among the princely eggs of the English eagle. This draws from Exeter the witless retort that 'it follows then the cat must stay at home'; and the zoological and metaphorical confusion is complete.

Oddly enough it is Hotspur from whom all the other cat (and kitten) allusions come. When Glendower boasts of the portents, fiery cressets, earthquakes or what have you, attending his nativity, Hotspur answers impatiently that these things would have happened at the same season if the Welshman's mother's cat had kittened and he himself had never been born: and it will be remembered that 'a ramping cat' is mentioned among the 'skimble-skamble' stuff of Merlin's prophecies as invoked by his braggart fellow-countryman. Most famous of all Shakespearean cats is surely Hotspur's kitten, invoked to emphasize his dislike of 'mincing poetry'.

> I had rather be a kitten and cry 'mew'
> Than one of these same metre ballad-mongers.

There are no cats in the Sonnets, but in *Lucrece* Tarquin is compared to 'a foul, night-walking cat'.

The master of New Place was not unaware of the little ways of the household cat. He observed that she lapped milk and stole cream: he had seen her with eyes of 'burning coal crouch before the mouse's hole': but, unlike Topsell, he has nothing to say about her loving nature to man; and she does not rub herself against the legs of any character in any of his plays. Rather may he have felt and remembered some sharp contact with her unsheathed claws, for Lysander, trying to escape from the clinging hands of Hermia, unkindly exclaims 'Hang off, thou cat, thou burr'.

However imperfect the affinity may have been between Shakespeare and the cat-family there was at least one place where he could not show his dislike of their society. This was the house of his early patron, Henry Wriothesley, Earl of Southampton. When this foppish and futile nobleman was imprisoned in the Tower for his complicity in the rebellion of Essex a limner came and painted him there, looking very wan and melancholy, but not utterly abandoned by man and beast. By his side sits an agreeable black-and-white cat, the manifest sharer of his solitude and comforter of his captivity.

Shakespeare knew all the current cat-proverbs of his time; that she had nine lives, that she was killed by care, that she let 'I dare not wait upon I would' when she wanted to catch fish without wetting her paws. There was another less familiar adage, 'Good liquor will make a cat speak'. Of this Stephano must have been thinking when he offered Caliban a sip from his bottle. 'Open your mouth: here is that which will give language to you, cat.'

Did the Elizabethans distinguish between *felis domestica* and the so-called civet cat, *viverra civetta*, from whom their favourite scent was obtained? 'Thou owest the worm no silk', says Lear to the disguised Edgar, 'the sheep no wool, the cat no perfume.' And he clamours to an invisible apothecary to give him an ounce of civet 'to sweeten his imagination'. Touchstone had other views. In the colloquy with Corydon on the question of court manners as contrasted with country manners, referring especially to the custom of hand-kissing, Corydon remarks that a shepherd's hands are often 'tarred over with the surgery of his sheep', whereas a courtier's are 'perfumed with civet'. Touchstone bids him 'learn of the wise and perpend'. Civet, he points out, 'is of a baser birth than tar, the very uncleanly flux of a cat'. I think we can deduce from this that, in common with most of his contemporaries, the poet believed that the civet was a member—even if an outlandish member—of the cat-tribe; and, further, that even when making himself ready to play before the Queen and her perfumed courtiers he never dipped his own fingers in an essence of such unpleasing provenance.

Unlike Shakespeare Philip Sidney was capable of taking a cat to his heart. Though he makes a passing allusion to an 'ugly cat' as being an unlucky thing to see, and though he associates the idea of melancholy with the cat family, he gives us in the *Arcadia*, during a dialogue between two most unconvincing swains named Nico and Pas, a delightful picture of his own pet.

> I have (and long shall have) a white, great nimble cat,
> A King upon a mouse, a strong foe to the rat.
> Fine eares, long taile he hath, with Lion's curbèd clawe,

Which oft he lifteth uy and stayes his lifted pawe.
Deep musing to himselfe, which after mewing showes,
Till with lickt bearde his eye of fire espie his foes.

The supposed association of cats with witchcraft goes very far back into the mists of time. Sacer to the Romans meant something dedicated and holy, something set apart; it also came to mean something wicked and horrible. This word spans the gulf between Bast the beneficent cat-headed goddess and the Graymalkin, the cat-shaped familiar spirit, to whom the First Witch in *Macbeth* exclaims 'I come'.

In Christendom the transition from the holy to the sinister was probably made by way of the religious recluses to whom even the most austere Rule allowed 'kat one' as a companion. After the Reformation, if not before, a solitary old woman, whether widow or spinster, upon whose desolate hearth a black cat sat purring was inevitably regarded as a witch. If her cat, after the fashion of the nicest kind of cat, came out to meet her, tail in air, when she hobbled back to her hovel with an armful of sticks to feed the fire so comforting to them both, if it thrust its head into her hand as she stooped to caress it, suspicion fell even more cruelly upon each of them.

The first words of the First Witch at the beginning of the cavern scene in *Macbeth* are 'Thrice the brindled cat hath mewed'; and we may be sure that the King for whose entertainment the play was written sat goggling happily as the Three Weird Sisters stirred their hellish brew. Shakespeare knew what he was about when he delved into Holinshed's Scottish Chronicles for a plot likely to appeal to a Scottish monarch who regarded himself as the world's greatest authority on witchcraft. Before we condemn James too harshly for his credulity, his obstinacy, and his share of the blame for the unspeakably cruel machinery which he helped to set in motion, we must see him against the background of his age, when nearly all men were credulous and cruel. If a rare spirit like Reginald Scot emerged from the crowd and wrote a book to show that the grimly-held current beliefs were 'Erroneous Novelties and Imaginary Conceptions', his ideas won few converts in England and were vigorously combated by parsons and others who should have known better. In Scotland, where witch-hunts were more frequent and more fierce, Scot's name was anathema: his *Discoverie of Witchcraft* was ordered to be burnt by the common hangman; and the King himself took up his royal quill to compose a refutation of these 'damnable opinions'. His *Daemonologie*, cast in the form of a colloquy between two pedantic bores, Philomathes,[2] who begins by being sceptical, and Epistemon,[3] who ends by convincing him, incidentally provided Shakespeare with further material for *Macbeth*.

It must be confessed that, all other things being equal, Epistemon found a very ingenious argument to support his views. 'Said not Samuell unto Saull that disobedience is as the sinne of Witchcraft? To compare to a thing that were not, it were too absurd.' We seem to catch a faint mew from Graymalkin when Philomathes wonders what can be the cause that there are twenty women given to that craft when there is one man. Epistemon has his answer pat. Women are more easily entrapped in the gross snares of the Devil, 'as was ower well proved to be true by the Serpent's deceiving Eva at the beginning, which makes him the homelier with that sex ever since'.

The King does not specifically allude to a familiar spirit in the form of a cat, but during those Trials for Witchcraft at which he presided he must have heard more than enough about these four-footed servants of Satan, and it must be acknowledged that the confession of Agnes Thompson of Haddington, 'the eldest witch of them all', gave him cause to look askance at reputed witches and to believe that a cat was frequently involved in their heathenish practices.

Having startled the King by repeating to him the very words which passed between him and the Queen on their wedding-night at Oslo in

The witch's sabbath, by Andries Jacobsz Stock, with a cat in the foreground.

Norway, the wretched crone admitted that by her arts she raised the storms which delayed the sailing of the King's ship 'at his cumming foorth of Denmark' with his bride and likewise the storm which wrecked another ship on its way from Burnt Island to the town of Leith with a cargo of 'sundrye Jewells and riche giftes' which should have been presented to the Queen on her arrival.

The method adopted by Agnes was as cruel as the process of 'swimming a witch', with its inevitable end—death. Let us listen to the story in her own words.[4]

—she confessed that at the time when His Majesty was in Denmark she, being accompanied by the parties before specially named,[5] took a Cat and christened it, and afterwards bound to each part of that Cat the chiefest parts of a dead man and several joints of his body, and that in the night following the said Cat was conveyed into the midst of the sea by all these witches sailing in their riddles or sieves as aforesaid, and so left the said Cat right before the Towne of Leith in Scotland. This done there did arise such a Tempest in the Sea as greater hath not been seen.

She then describes the loss of the vessel with the jewels intended for the new Queen. But worse remained behind.

Again it is confessed that the said christened Cat was the cause that the King's Majesty's Ship at his coming forth from Denmark had a contrary wind to the rest of his ships, then being in his company, which thing was most strange and true, as the King's Majesty acknowledgeth, for when the rest of the Ships had a fair and good wind, then was the wind contrary and altogether against His Majesty.

It may well be asked why, when Agnes Thompson and her sinister sisterhood had thus set roaring war betwixt the green sea and the azured vault, they did not contrive to wreck the ship carrying the King whom their master, Satan, recognized as the greatest enemy that he had in the world. We soon learn why they failed.

—and further the said Witch declared that His Majesty would never have come safely from the sea if his faith had not prevailed above their intentions.

Shakespeare's contemporaries also introduced witches and cats into their plays, one very often temporarily incarnate in the other. Heywood, for example, in *The Witches of Lancashire*, takes us to a haunted Mill, and brings upon the scene a Miller with scratched and bloody hands. 'Cats do you call them?' exclaims the victim, 'for their hugeness they might be cat-a-mountains. Good landlord, provide yourself with a new tenant. I'll not endure such another night if you would give me your Mill for nothing.' A stout-hearted soldier volunteers to take over the Mill; but he, too, has an unquiet night, harassed by the witches. When he 'stops their caterwauling with his bilbo' and cuts off what he took to be a cat's paw, he finds that it is the hand of Mrs Generous, a crypto-witch.

Learned persons disagree as to the exact date when Thomas Middleton's *The Witch* was written, and are not of one mind as to the relationship between this rather lurid drama and *Macbeth*; one thing at least is certain. We meet more cats in Middleton than in Shakespeare. One of the Witch's familiars is named 'Kit-with-the-Candlestick'; a spirit in the form of a cat descends to demand her dues—a kiss and a sip of blood before the sisterhood flies away over steeples, turrets and towers. 'The Cat sings a brave treble in her own language', comments Firebrace, the Witch's son; and he later remarks, 'I know as well as can be when my Mother's mad and our great cat angry, for one spits French then, and the other spits Latin.'

It was not necessary profanely to christen nor cruelly to drown any cat in order to raise a wind. The power was implicit in them all. Sometimes they would exert it when annoyed, from which it seems to follow that Graymalkin might on occasion do the same thing to oblige a friend.

If we grope (rather uncomfortably) for the reason underlying the various cruelties inflicted on the cat in the days of Shakespeare, we may possibly find it in this general and popular identification of the poor thing with the imps of Satan. Her faculty of seeing in the dark, the expanding and contracting of the pupils of the eyes, her indomitable dignity, her solemn deportment, all the attributes, indeed, which made her seem sacred to the Ancient Egyptians were now interpreted to her undoing.

It is curious to remark that many centuries after the spread of Christianity might have been expected to weaken, if not to obliterate, the hideous streak of cruelty that seems to lodge in the human sub-consciousness, that streak remained.

The owner of the Casa del Fauno, Pompeii, in the first century AD found pleasure in the mosaic picture of a cat clutching a terrified domestic

An early witchcraft woodcut.

fowl. Sixteen hundred years would pass before Mary, Queen of Scots, busy with the hangings which she and her gaoleress, Bess of Shrewsbury, sat embroidering together, would choose to trace with her needle the likeness of a truly grim Graymalkin, bushy-whiskered and glaring-eyed.[6] This 'catte' (as Mary has carefully labelled her) sits in a prim attitude, gazing straight ahead: but the kink at the top of her tail suggests that it is beginning to twitch in a manner that bodes ill to the cylindrical rodent (more like a rat than a mouse) stealing away to the right of the spectator.

Two more centuries stream by and we see the four charming children of Admiral Lord George Graham as painted by William Hogarth. In the foreground one little girl dances to the music of a bird-organ of which her brother turns the handle; another holds the plump fist of the youngest of the three, who sits in a low wheeled chair and is obviously enchanted with the thrilling notes of the organ. Did those notes drown the frantic cheeping of the caged bird in the background and the desperate fluttering of its wings? Well might the poor captive flutter. A large tabby cat is peering at it over the back of a chair, teeth bared and green eyes aglow.

Sailors are humane men as a rule. The father of these little Scots was painted by Hogarth in his cabin, with a pet dog upon whose head he

Mary, Queen of Scots' Embroidered 'Catte'. *By courtesy of the Duke of Hamilton, K.T., and the Holyrood Amenities Trust*

has playfully clapped his own wig. It is difficult to understand how he could bear to have that glimpse of grinning jaws and beating feathers introduced in this gay group of children. If the idea was Hogarth's and not his, it is even more difficult to understand how Lord George came to give it his approval.

Nobody with an exposed nerve in the mind where cruelty is concerned would willingly linger over the barbarities practised upon cats and other animals in the Golden Age of England. The onlookers enjoyed it all prodigiously. Was there also an element of sadistic glee in the 'Puritane one' at Banbury who was seen

> Hanging of his cat on Monday
> For killing of a rat on Sunday?

It seems at least possible.

# The Witch's Familiar— More Literary Cats, French and English

The 'Puritane One' appeared in Richard Braithwaite's *Barnabae Itinerarium* on the eve of the Civil War. In the year of Shakespeare's death Thomas Tomkins of Trinity College, Cambridge, wrote a play entitled *Patho-Machia or the Battell of the Affections*, where he introduces us to certain 'factious men'

> whereof one of late killed his cat because it
> killed a Mouse on Sunday.

The joke was circulating well into the seventeenth century. Thomas Master, friend and literary assistant of Lord Herbert of Cherbury, inserts it into his fantastic little poem, *Lute-Strings Cat-Eaten*. His cat had come in the silence of the night and gnawed the strings of his ivory-inlaid lute until only a few pathetic shreds remained. He will curse her for it. May she dwell with 'some dry hermit', where 'rat ne'er peeped, where mouse ne'er fed', or with some 'close-pared brother' with whom she must either fast on Sunday or else be hanged the day after. Perhaps Puss was melancholy, and wanted to cheer herself with music. She was obviously a favourite to whom anything might be forgiven.

Robert Herrick was very far from being a 'close-pared brother', and there was no fast-day for the Parsonage cat at Dean Prior.

> A cat
> I keep that plays about my house Grown fat
> With eating many a miching mouse.

A portly cat is seldom playful, but Herrick's may have kept herself in condition by the constant pursuit of the miching mice.

Belief in witchcraft, in witches and their familiars, died hard in England, but it was never so strong as to deter people from keeping down the mouse-population in the traditional way. The hearth-cat, whether lying upon a Turkish carpet in the withdrawing-room or upon the warm flagstones before the kitchen fire, was a creature whom none feared and many loved. Kind hands set cream before her sometimes: milk and fish were never lacking; and when a kettle with a lid and a spout came into common use there came into existence that cosiest of all double sounds, a singing kettle and a purring cat.

Very different was the fate of the cat whose mistress was condemned as a witch. A cat? No, a familiar spirit, an evil thing, and as such deserving death. Usually it was a black animal upon whom suspicion fell; but the colour of one was indicated by its name in the indictment: 'White Kitling'.

That grotesque and horrible person, Matthew Hopkins, was the first official Witch Finder General of England. Another 'Puritan one', and much encouraged by the Independents and the Anabaptists, he sent hundreds of hapless old women to death, and, it is to be feared, often doomed their four-footed friends with them. In the frontispiece to his *Discovery of Witches* (1647) five familiars are seen in attendance on two witches. Of these five two are fantastic monsters, one is a black hare named 'Sacke and Sugar', one a rat-like creature called 'Newes', and only one unmistakably a cat. Perhaps it is a kitten. The witch stretches her hand towards it, and it approaches her with confidence, tail in air, when she addresses it as 'Holt'. Matthew Hopkins stands in the background, watching them narrowly. Poor Holt by showing thus plainly upon what good terms he was with his mistress may have sealed her fate—and his own.

Though the Puritans were great pursuers of witches it should not be forgotten that one year before Hopkins's horrid book appeared, a Puritan parson, John Gaule, sickened by the persecution growing and spreading in England, particularly in his own territory of East Anglia, published a collection of his sermons on witchcraft—a courageous action, for a man who questioned the existence of this branch of Satan's activities laid himself open to the charge of being himself a 'collaborator'. 'Every old woman', says Gaule, 'with a wrinkled face, a hairy lip, a squint eyes, a spindle in her hand, and a dog or a cat by her side, is not only suspected but pronounced for a witch.'

Witches with their familiars from Matthew Hopkins' *Discovery of Witches*, 1647.

Witchcraft was not, as far as I am aware, among the crimes laid to Archbishop Laud's charge, but, to borrow an expressive modern idiom, his enemies would not have 'put it past him', especially if they heard that in his palace at Lambeth he cherished a family of 'parti-coloured cats' and more sinister still—'took great delight in their company'. Those inscrutable creatures, stalking sedately in the wake of the abhorred Anglican robes, and in their rich colours rivalling the copes and chasubles which were an abomination to all godly men, must surely have seemed an only-too-appropriate retinue for the Anti-Christ of Canterbury.

John Aubrey remarks that the Archbishop was 'a great lover of Catts', and that he was presented with some 'Cypruss' or tabby cats, which were 'sold at first for £5 a piece'. It is an interesting point that tabbies are called 'Cyprus cats' in Norfolk to this day.

Samuel Pepys, future President of the Royal Society, was once credulous enough to imagine—though only for a moment and in usual circumstances—that his 'young Gib cat' might be a spirit.

At 7 a.m. on the morning of 29 November 1667, Mr and Mrs Pepys were roused from their slumbers by some undoubtedly peculiar noises— knockings, sounds as of furniture being moved about, footsteps, as it seemed, going up and down the stairs.

> We lay both of us afeared: yet I would have rose, but my wife would not let me. Besides, I could not do it without making a noise, and we

A woodcut of a witch feeding her cat, with toads to the side.

did both conclude that thieves were in the house, but wondered what our people did, whom we thought either killed or afeared as we were.

Thus we lay till the clock struck eight and high day . . .

At last Mr Pepys rose, pulled on his breeches, wrapped his gown about him, took a firebrand in his hand—and opened the bedroom-door. The noise had now ceased, and there was nothing to be seen. He then roused Jane, the maid, who confessed that she, too, had been 'afeared'; but, more stout-hearted than their master, she and a fellow-servant had got up to investigate. They found nothing stirring except the cook, already at her post in the kitchen.

It was Jane, apparently, who pointed out that the mysterious din proceeded from the great chimneystack of Sir John Minnes' house next door. 'So we sent', records Pepys, 'and their chimneys have been swept this morning, and the noise was that and nothing else.' The episode, he declares, is one of the most extraordinary accidents in his life. He is reminded of Don Quixote's adventures; and as he ends the chronicle of the day he reveals what it was that had made him and his Elizabeth rather inclined to feel 'afeared' in its early hours.

> Last night our Gib-cat did leap down our stairs from top to bottom at two leaps, and frighted us that we could not tell whether it was a cat or a spirit, and do sometimes think this morning that the house might be haunted.

The nature of the visitation suggests a *poltergeist*, though the sounds might have proceeded from the clanking of ghostly fetters. If it were not for the widely-held belief that no cat was afraid of any ghost, Pepys might have concluded that his young Gib, instead of being a spirit, had itself been frightened by a visitant from another sphere.

Calvinistic preoccupation with witchcraft crossed the Atlantic in the company of the Pilgrim Fathers, coloured their ideas, darkened their judgement, and led to the notorious Witch-Hunts at Salem, Massachusetts. To his honour be it recorded, Increase Mather, the Anglo-American divine, did what he could to stem the tide of credulity and cruelty which swept over New England in the last decades of the seventeenth century; but the time was not ripe for tolerance, and his son, Cotton Mather, was both an instigator and encourager of the notorious persecutions, which lasted into the eighteenth century.

A young Englishman, one Richard Chamberlayn[1] of Gray's Inn, was staying in the house of a planter named George Walter, in the province of 'New Hampshire', when the Terror was within a few years of extinction. His sojourn coincided with a remarkable outbreak of what he learnedly describes as *Lithobolia*, or the 'throwing of stones'. These objects are reported to have showered, rolled and pattered all over the place. Mr Chamberlayn's narrative is so charming that it deserves to be quoted verbatim—in part, at least.

> In the Evening, as soon as I had supped in the outer room before mine, I took a little Musical Instrument and began to touch it (the door indeed was set open for Air) and a good big stone came rumbling in and as it were to lead the dance, but upon a much different Account than in days of Old and of old, fabulous Enchantments, my Musick being none of the best.
>
> The Noise of this[2] brought up the Deputy-President's Wife and many others of the neighbourhood who were below, who wondered to see this Stone followed, as it were, by many others and a Pewter Spoon among the rest. . . . And beside all this there was seen by two Youths in the Orchard and Fields, as they said, a black Cat at the time the Stones were tossed about, and it was shot at and missed by its changing Places and being immediately at some distance and then out of sight, as they related.

Mr Chamberlayn, as befitted a member of the Honourable Society of Gray's Inn, was careful to distinguish between what he had heard and what he had seen. He thinks the alleged presence of the black Cat near the house where *Lithobolia* was going on deserved to be noted: but he says nothing about familiar spirits, and has no theories to account for the phenomena. Any cat, black, white, ginger or tabby, has always been capable of 'changing Places and being immediately at some distance'. A hundred years earlier we might have been solemnly told that she had been hit, and that a track of bloody paw-marks had led straight to the house where a suspected Witch, now restored to her human form, lay dying.

Very different from the haggard 'familiar' of that suspected witch was the Roman cat whose portrait is preserved in the Palazzo Braschi. 'A lordly and imposing creature', Mr H. V. Morton calls it. Black and white in colour, demure yet alert, he sits on a tasselled cushion wearing a broad collar sewn with small bells. Attached to the curtain behind him is a poem recording that a great and beautiful lady once kissed this *amabel Gatto*, bade him keep his heart pure, and charged him to remember her kiss, 'even in the next world'.

In spite of the traditional association with witches and spinsters, the cat seems always to have been a greater favourite with men than with women. Is this because of her essential femininity? Among the famous men who savoured her society was Montaigne. His cat alone was freely admitted to that tower which he built for himself as a refuge from all human contacts. She was his playmate as well as his companion:

> When I am playing with my Cat who knows whether she have more sport in dallying with me than I have in gaming with her? We entertain one another with mutual apish tricks. If I have my hour to begin or refuse, so hath she hers.[3]

There seems always to have been a natural affinity between philosophers and cats. Sir Thomas Browne cherished several, who were observed in the garden of his house at Norwich by the learned and eminent persons who sought him out there.

Montaigne's disciple, his 'accomplished Female Friend',[4] Marie de Gournay, shared his love of cats. When, long after his death, she published a pamphlet advocating the perpetuation, or even the resuscitation, of antique words and terms in the French language, St Evremond wrote a satirical play poking fun at her, and Cardinal Richelieu had the bad taste to pay her a mocking compliment in obsolete phrases taken from her own works.

'You are laughing at a poor old woman', she told the Cardinal, 'But laugh on—everyone must be made to contribute to your diversion.'

Slightly abashed, His Eminence actually begged her pardon. Later he told his friend, the Abbé de Boisrobert, that he wished something to be done for her. She must have a pension of 200 crowns a year. The Abbé mentioned that Mademoiselle de Gournay kept a manservant. 'Let him have 50 livres a year,' said the Cardinal. Then there is Madame Paillan,[5] her cat. 'I give *her* 20 livres a year on condition that she has kittens.' 'Monseigneur, she *has* had kittens.' The Cardinal, who was clearly in a giving humour, added another pistole for the kittens.

Pope's famous phrase about the lady who might 'die and endow a college or a cat' was long supposed to refer to 'La Belle Stuart' otherwise Frances Theresa, Duchess of Richmond and Lennox.

A view of Alexander Pope's villa at Twickenham by Samuel Scott.

The poet himself must have had her in his mind, and indeed she was a lady round whom legends gathered, legends of her beauty, her virtue, and her love for birds and animals. Generations of visitors to the Wax Effigies at Westminster Abbey have been told that she left instructions in her Will that her faithful grey parrot should be stuffed and placed on a perch beside her image, and there indeed it sits: but we find no word about it in her Will, nor is there any mention of the annuities which she was believed to have bequeathed to certain poor gentlewomen 'on condition that they took care of her cats'. Pope was a small, ailing five-year-old when the lovely Frances died, but he must have known people who remembered her, and it was probably from these people that he learned the cat legend. Alas, it was a legend only; neither cat nor parrot is specifically named in her last Testament. The annuities were real enough, however; many poor relations, needy ladies and old servants received them, and it is more than likely that she left some verbal directions concerning her cats to legatees who shared (or perhaps pretended to share?) her love for them.

Pope has not immortalized any cat of his own as he immortalized his dog 'Bounce', but one cannot imagine the Villa at Twickenham without a Pussy, and his mother was just the sort of old lady who would be happiest with one somewhere about. It is perhaps not without significance that in his *Imitations of Horace*, when he handles the fable of the Town Mouse and the Country Mouse,[6] a cat is introduced for whom there is no warrant in the Latin text.

> 'A Rat! A Rat! Clap to the door!'
> The Cat comes bouncing on the floor.

'Bouncing' is an excellent description of the springy, seesaw motion characteristic of a suddenly alerted cat, pursuing but not yet ready to pounce.

The visual conjunction between the toothless crone and the faithful 'familiar' was maintained all through the eighteenth century, and well into the nineteenth.[7] As Mr Spectator was walking one day with Sir Roger de Coverley they met an aged woman who begged alms from the visitor. After they had gone on their way the good old Knight remarked that she had the reputation of a witch all over the country and that:

> there was not a Switch about her house which her neighbours did not believe had carried her several hundreds of miles'. Sticks were laid cross-wise in her path. If she made a mistake at church and said 'Amen' in the wrong place she was suspected of saying her prayers backwards. Her name was Moll White, and the countryside rang with the exploits ascribed to her. 'This account', remarked Mr Spectator, 'raised my curiosity so far that I begged my friend Sir Roger to go with me into her hovel, which stood in a solitary corner under the side of the wood. Upon our first entering Sir Roger winked to me and pointed at something that stood behind the door which upon looking that was I discovered to be an old broomstaff. At the same time he whispered me in the ear to take notice of a tabby cat that sat in the chimney-corner which, as the old knight told me, lay under as bad a report as Moll White herself, for besides that Moll was said often to accompany her in the same shape, the cat is reported to have spoken twice or thrice in her life and to have played several pranks above the capacity of an ordinary cat.

The Fabulists of the English Augustan Age did not neglect poor Pussy. John Gay's Twenty-First Fable tells of a house grievously plundered by rats and of a housemaid, Betty, who 'cursed the Cat for want of duty'. A professional Rat-Catcher was then engaged, a 'man of wondrous skill',

Alexander Pope, (1688-1744), by Charles Jervas.

who planned his campaign with care, sought out the habits and the haunts of the pests, and proceeded to lay his well-baited traps in all the likeliest places.

The dispossessed cat followed him round, perceiving that if he should flourish

> The purring race must be undone.

She thought she knew a trick worth two of that, and secretly removed the bait from every trap.

Finding himself thus frustrated, the Vermin Exterminator (as he would now demand to be called) proceeded to counter-measures. He brought a pondrous trap of unusual size, baited it with judgment—and succeeded in catching the cat. In vain she mewed piteously for pardon; in vain she pleaded that he should spare 'a sister of the science'. He retorted, unmoved, that if the whole of her 'interloping band' were banished his calling would raise its fees and, indeed, establish a monopoly.

At this point an older and wiser cat intervened with a powerful argument. Two of a trade, she observes, have never agreed. Squires, beauties, kings, all envy and assail each other. Why should not cats and rat-catchers show greater wisdom, limit their desires, and accept the fact that there is 'game' enough for them all? The fable ends there: but one may hope that the Rat-Catcher was convinced, and that the 'ponderous trap' opened its jaws at last.

The familiar figure of the cat-attended crone reappears in Gay's Twenty-Third Fable. We see her sitting in 'a little smoky flame', mumbling her prayers backwards and surrounded by lank and mewing cats. Annoyed by their din, the 'untamed scold of fourscore years' most unfairly rounds on them and bids them be gone. If they had not been 'housed and nursed', she would never have been pursued by yelling boys, crossed straws would not have been laid athwart her path, horseshoes would not have been nailed to the doors of houses to protect the inhabitants from her spells, nor would the wenches have hidden away their brooms 'for fear that she might up and ride'. One of the cats has a retort ready. If they had not lived meagrely beneath her roof they could have lived 'with credit' as 'beasts of chase'.

> 'Tis infamy to serve a hag;
> Cats are thought imps, her broom a nag;

> And boys against our lives combine
> Because 'tis thought *your* cats have nine.

Gay here betrays some ignorance of the habits of the cat. Unless the hag kept her locked in the hovel there was nothing to prevent her from going forth to hunt.

In the Augustan Age as in every other the fabulist leaned heavily upon the animal endowed with the gift of human speech. Edward Moore, in the ninth of the fables which he dedicated to Caroline of Anspach, Princess of Wales, describes a 'jolly farmer' seated at table and sharing titbits with his favourite spaniel. When in her turn the cat seeks a share, the dog protests that

> They only earn a right to eat
> Who earn by services their meat.

He waxes eloquent on the theme of his own exertions, springing and retrieving the game, defending his master's flock from wolves and his house from robbers.

The cat, with quite uncatlike meekness, owns the 'superior merit' of the dog; but she pleads that she contributes to the well-being of man as far as she can. Who destroys the pilfering mouse? Who keeps the farm free from vermin? Who protects 'the labouring swain' from the rats who would otherwise have wrought havoc in the granary? (A terrier could have done this quite as well, if not better; but apparently the only dog in the landscape is of another breed.) Much impressed, the farmer declares that her words are just, and spurns the 'snarler' from his side.

Midway between Æsop and Gay stands the anonymous author of the French *fabliaux*: and in this company of satirically-conceived beasts it is obvious that a cat must needs be numbered. So here he is, Sir Tibert by name, soft-spoken, sly, but sometimes strangely gullible. He is no match for Reynard the Fox.

When the little dog Curtois complains to King Noble, the Lion, that Reynard had filched from him the 'one poor pudding' which in a bitter winter season was 'all the meat he had', Sir Tibert, probably from dislike of Curtois rather than love of Reynard, ranges himself on the side of the delinquent. What beast is there who would not find it difficult to excuse all his past actions? The theft of the pudding is old history now. 'I myself', adds Tibert, 'make no complaint, yet the pudding in question happened to be mine. I took it by night out of a mill, while the miller lay slumbering.'

The other animals take Tibert's championship of Reynard in very ill part. It is resolved that the fox shall be summoned to appear before the King and that the cat, 'for his gravity and wisdom', shall carry the summons. Sir Tibert does not much like his errand. He protests that he is 'little and feeble', and thinks that the bear, the 'noble Sir Bruin', should be sent instead. Whereto the Lion makes answer, 'It is for your wisdom, Sir Tibert, that I employ you, not for your strength.' Reynard, standing at the door of his castle of Malepardus, greets his cousin Tibert kindly and readily agrees to accompany him to court; but he would rather not travel by moonlight. Let them wait till morning. In the meantime he hospitably offers a supper of honeycomb. Tibert answers that, for his part, he would rather have a mouse for supper than all the honeycomb in Christendom.

'A mouse?' says Reynard. 'Why, cousin, there dwelleth a priest hard by whose barn is so stuffed with rats and mice that I think half the wagons in the parish could not hold them all.'

Tibert answers, in the manner of Bertram Wooster, 'Lead me to it.'

Well did Reynard know that the priest, from whom he had filched a fat hen the previous night, had set a trap for him in a promising position. Tibert yields to Reynard's prompting, and leaps through the gap in the farmyard wall, thoughtfully pointed out to him. The trap closes; he is held fast; and when he mews piteously the fox asks him cynically if it is 'court fashion' to sing with one's meat.

Roused by the din, the priest and all his household fall upon poor Sir Tibert, and Reynard, regarding his 'cousin' as practically dead already, steals back to Malepardus well content.

But Sir Tibert, being a cat, is not so easily killed. He breaks out of the snare, gnaws his way through the cord pinioning him, jumps through the hole in the wall, and creeps, 'roaring and stumbling', back to the Court of King Noble.

When at last Reynard does appear before the King to answer for his many misdeeds, he pleads that 'as for Tibert' he had received him with all friendship, and it was not his fault if, in spite of his warning, the cat had insisted on creeping into the priest's barn in quest of mice. But he is none the less condemned to be hanged.

Tibert runs to the gibbet with the halter in his mouth, makes a running noose, and eagerly assists Isegrim the Wolf in the final preparations.

At the eleventh hour Reynard contrives to persuade King Noble that all the animals who had borne witness against him were secretly conspiring to kill the King. In the ensuing episodes, the pilgrimage to Rome and the trial by combat, Tibert has no conspicuous part to play; but after Reynard has defeated Isegrim in the Lists we catch a glimpse of the cat aiding Dame Ereswine, the victim's wife, and Bruin the Bear, his friend, to cover him with hay to keep him warm, and to bind up his wounds which number no fewer than twenty-five.

Though it was in the reign of Louis XIV that Charles Perrault set down the old folk-tale 'Englished' under the title of *Puss-in-Boots*, the action and the atmosphere are those of the *fabliaux*, and we seem to be listening to a narrator in the days of St Louis. No fairies intervene; nobody explains how the gift of human speech descended upon the cat which was the good miller's only legacy to the youngest of his three sons; but the cunning, the resourcefulness and the audacity of the animal are strongly reminiscent of Reynard, though with this important difference, that they are exercised for his young master's benefit, not for his own.

La Fontaine, whether borrowing from the early fabulists or using his own inventive powers, is often more sophisticated in his approach; yet he no less than his forerunners is keenly conscious of the value of a cat

Puss in Boots by Gustav Doré.

as an actor in a fable. Take, for example, *The Cock, the Cat and the Little Mouse.*

The mouse, a very young and ingenuous mouselet, came running to its mother to describe two strange creatures whom he had just encountered. One was graceful and benignant-looking; the other, active and alarming. This second beast had a shrill, fierce voice, two arm-like things with which he beat the air, a tail like a flaunting knightly plume, and a piece of flesh on the top of his head. The little mouse would have fled from this outlandish being had he not felt reassured by the presence of the more amiable stranger, whose fur was as soft as his own, who was prettily striped, had a long tail, and bore on its face a mild, modest expression, though its eyes certainly did glow. Moreover, it seemed well disposed towards mice, and the bold infant would have spoken to it had not a sudden blare of noise from 'the other' sent him scurrying away. 'My son,' then said the Mother Mouse, 'that gentle creature was a cat. Under its hypocritical airs it nourishes an inextinguishable feud against all our

A conversation piece set in the great cabin of the vessel which took Lord Boyne from Venice to Lisbon. Gustavus Hamilton succeeded to the title in 1723 and shortly before coming of age he made the Grand Tour. Note the cat under the table, is this the ship's cat or a special cat?

family. Your "other", on the contrary, far from doing us any harm, may someday provide us with a dinner, for he is a cock. As for your cat, it is we who would do the providing.'

> *Moral:*
> As long as you may live beware
> Of judging people by their air.

# Dr Johnson—Horace Walpole— Thomas Gray—Christopher Smart—Cat-Lovers All

It was in the eighteenth century that the conscious cat-lover came into his own. Think only of Dr Johnson, Horace Walpole, Thomas Gray, Christopher Smart, to whom must be added William Cowper. Cats became individuals rather than types. We can now detect the varying notes of their purrs. Sometimes we are advised very particularly of their colours. Often they have some trick of movement or of mood which sets them apart from the vague mass of mouse-chasing, milk-lapping, fish-filching, comfort-loving creatures. They may be involved in little comedies or tragedies that have left an enduring mark on literature.

No kitchen can ever have been complete without its cat—not even the earliest medieval kitchen with its bubbling cauldrons, its spit revolving before a fierce open fire, its brass basins scoured till they looked like the golden locks of a fair lady. Where straw and rushes were thickly strewn mice and rats would abound, and an active Gib would not be lacking to keep their numbers down. But it seems to have been late in the day that the cat, for all her elegance of form and habit, was admitted to the solar chamber where little dogs were welcomed with so much indulgence. As for the great hall, where many a delicious morsel of carp or venison might confidently be expected to fall from the table, it is the lap-dog and not—if one may coin a phrase—the lap-cat who is depicted lurking hopefully below. The bedchamber was another matter.[1]

In the Georgian period we find a more just appreciation of the cat's graces and merits, and a more powerful concentration of literary allusions is focused upon her. It was a carpeted and cushioned age, well adapted to please her feline ladyship. At least four of its men of letters were sealed of her tribe, and these four, being lightly linked together, are remembered in the present chapter. A possible fifth, William Cowper to wit, will follow in the next. In his instance it will be suggested that the seal is less powerfully impressed. They form a sharply-contrasted quartette, these Augustan cat-lovers. The contrast is thrown into high relief when we try to catch a fleeting glimpse of them through each other's eyes. Horace Walpole, for example, called Dr Johnson a 'saucy Caliban', and firmly refused to allow Sir Joshua Reynolds to introduce them at a Royal Academy banquet. In conversation with Boswell, Johnson conceded that 'Horry Walpole' had 'got together a great many curious little things and told them in an elegant manner'; but a political chasm yawned between them deeper than any divide made by habit, personality or deportment. The great Tory who, when concocting Parliamentary speeches for the *Gentleman's Magazine*, 'always took care to put Sir Robert Walpole in the wrong' could hardly be expected to praise the lord of Strawberry Hill, or to be praised by him. Did he not roll a dubious eye upon the Rev. James Grainger's *Biographical History* merely because he was patronized by the younger Walpole? And Gray he dismissed as being 'dull in a new way which made many people think him great'.

Gray made the acquaintance of Christopher Smart when they were both Fellows of Pembroke College, Cambridge; he started several efforts to befriend him; but it is to be feared that he did in the end find the poor fellow 'an unmitigated nuisance';[2] Smart, however, admired 'our great Augustan Gray'; and Johnson refused to regard 'Kit' as being crazy merely because he insisted on people praying with him and did not love clean linen.

'I'd as lief pray with Kit Smart as anyone else', said the Doctor; and in a burst of candour he avowed that for clean linen he himself had 'no passion'.

Here, then, are the four Augustans between whom there was one strong bond of sympathy: their common love of cats. Horace Walpole coined the excellent word, 'dogmanity'; he might have added 'catmanity' as a pendant. Himself he was one of those agreeable people who can divide their hearts in fairly equal portions between the dog and the cat; but Johnson, who had so much in him of the surly yet faithful type of dog, was quite clearly a cat-man.

When that uncouth dominie set up house with his red-cheeked Tetty it is impossible to doubt that a cat completed the domestic group at Edial. It is equally impossible to doubt that there was a cat resident in

Dr Johnson, was a cat lover. It was whilst he was in residence at 17 Gough Square that he owned his most well-known cat, Hodge. A bronze statue of Hodge, appropriately seated on a dictionary, forms part of a memorial to Johnson at the far end of the square.

Gough Square when the Dictionary was produced and where this terse definition was written:

> CAT: a domestick animal that catches mice, commonly reckoned by naturalists the lowest order of the leonine species.

At the time that James Boswell ran the Doctor to earth, first at Mr Davies' book-shop in Russell Street, Covent Garden, and then in darkling chambers on a first floor in Inner Temple Lane, a cat, or possibly even more than one, formed part of the untidy, probably mouse-haunted, household. In this careful description of his preliminary call upon his idol, Boswell does not mention their presence. As he was constitutionally antipathetic to cats he could hardly have failed to record the unavoidable shudder which would have attended the sudden appearance of a member of the tribe on that memorable occasion.

The ordeal was not, however, very long deferred. It was impossible to frequent Johnson's formidable company without catching an occasional bright glimpse of the two most engaging aspects of his character, his love of children ('pretty dears') and his love of cats. 'I shall never', wrote Boswell,

> forget the indulgence with which he treated Hodge, his cat, for whom he himself used to go out and buy oysters lest the servants, having that trouble, should take a dislike to the poor creature.

Who opened those oysters for Hodge? Who tipped them all slithery and delicious, on to a platter and placed them on the floor? The answer is clearly Dr Johnson himself.

> 'I am', writes Boswell, 'unluckily one of those who have an antipathy to a cat, so that I am uneasy when in the room with one; and I own I frequently suffered a good deal from the presence of this same Hodge. I recollect him one day scrambling up Dr Johnson's breast, apparently with much satisfaction, while my friend, smiling and half whistling, rubbed down his back and pulled him by the tail.'

Either Boswell studiously concealed from his friend his constitutional dislike of cats or has concealed from us the Doctor's comments upon what he must have regarded as an unamiable quirk which a man of

Johnson (1775) showing his intense concentration and the weakness of his eyes; he did not want to be depicted as 'Blinking Sam'.

James Boswell at the age of 25.

common sensibility ought to have been able to overcome. The word 'allergy' was not in the great Dictionary; the phenomenon had as yet no name.

As he sat watching Hodge enthroned upon Johnson's mighty and maculate waistcoat Mr Boswell made an effort which—in view of his presumed sensations at the time must be regarded as an almost heroic one. He remarked that it was a fine cat.

'Why, yes, Sir,' announced the Doctor, 'but I have had cats whom I have liked better than this'; and then as if perceiving Hodge to be out of countenance, adding, 'but he is a very fine cat, a very fine cat indeed.'

The 'other cats' whom Johnson had 'liked better' must indeed have been near to his heart, for this immortal incident reminded Boswell of the ludicrous account which he gave to Bennet Langton of 'a young Gentleman of good family'.

> 'Sir, when I heard of him last he was running about town shooting cats.' And then, in a sort of kindly reverie, he bethought himself of his own favourite cat and said, 'But Hodge shan't be shot: no, no, Hodge shall not be shot.'

Horace Walpole was a dog-lover almost from infancy; but neither dogs nor cats are specifically named among the 'cruatuars' who he was glad (at the age of eight) to hear were 'all wall'. His catmanity was perhaps of a more gradual growth than his dogmanity. There is not much enthusiasm in his first response to Lord Islay's quest of a pair of the Maltese breed in the year 1741. Shortly after Walpole's return to London from the Italian tour made memorable both by the beginning of his friendship with Sir Horace Mann and the near-ending of his friendship with Gray, this eccentric sprig of the Clan Cambell[3] dined at Arlington Street with Sir Robert. Young Mr Walpole happened to excite the guest's interest by mentioning the fine Maltese cats bred by an ambiguous Prussian exile called Stosch, who was a bit of a virtuoso, a suspected Jacobite spy and 'a man of the most infamous character in every respect'.

Always complaisant, Walpole communicated at once with Sir Horace Mann:

> Lord Islay begged I would write to Florence to have the largest male and female that could be got. If you will speak to Stosch you will oblige me. They may come by sea.

Philip Mercier, The Sense of Touch, 1744–47. The lap cat steals the central scene in the painting.

In May of the ensuing year he wrote to the same faithful correspondent:

> I laughed very much at the family of cats I am to receive. I believe they will be extremely welcome to Lord Islay, for he appears little, lives more darkly and more like a wizard than ever. These huge cats will figure prodigiously in his cell.

Two months later they were 'those odious cats of Malta', not because of any intrinsic demerits but because their acquisition and despatch to England were giving Mann an unconscionable amount of trouble. Now, however, Walpole's soft spot for all animals betrays itself. His mind misgives him.

> Oh, the cats! I can never keep them, and yet it is barbarous to send them all to Lord Islay. He will shut them up and starve them, and then bury them under the stairs with his wife.

Horace Walpole, (1717-1797), by John Giles *c.* 1755.

This macabre burial—if it ever took place at all—must have occurred when Walpole himself was only six years old; but we know that as a child he had lent an attentive ear to the gossip of his mother's waiting-women, and it may well be that some such legend was whispered among the Abigails at Chelsea where the Walpole family was living during the first stage of Sir Robert's last, long tenure of office.

In November, 1743, the Maltese cats, number unspecified, were still a theme of conjecture. 'The poor Maltese cats', wrote Walpole, 'never arrived here.' And thereafter we hear no more of them.

During the interval between their first and last appearance in the correspondence Sir Robert had fallen from power, had accepted the earldom of Orford, and had been obliged to transfer himself and his family from Downing Street to his great palace at Houghton, pending the acquisition of a suitable town house.

In July, 1742, young Horace was 'up to his ears in packing'. He told Mann that he looked like St John in the Isle of Patmos, writing Revelations and prophesying, 'Woe! Woe! Woe! The Kingdom of Desolation is at hand.' But he added characteristically,

> Indeed I have prettier animals about me than he ever dreamt of: here is dear Patapan and a little Van Dyke cat with black whiskers and boots; you would swear it was of a very ancient family in the West of England, famous for their loyalty.

The beginning of the next year—1743—found him installed in his father's recently acquired house in Arlington Street, destined to be his own London home for some thirty-seven years. With him he had of course brought from Norfolk all his 'baubles and Patapans and cats'.

Lord Orford died in March, 1745, bequeathing his London house to his youngest son, and in that house there occurred an event destined indirectly to lead to one of the most famous cat-poems in the English language: namely, the reconciliation between Horace and his former schoolfellow, Thomas Gray, from whom he had parted in anger at Reggio four and a half years earlier.

They did not recover the lost territories of friendship very easily; but once on the old, familiar footing they learned to tolerate each other's foibles and prize each other's good qualities better than before.

The 'little tub of forty pounds a year' which Walpole rented at Windsor in the summer of 1746 was merely an ante-room to the famous

Villa at Strawberry Hill which became his some twelve months later. But it was not without attractions. It was within sight of Eton, almost within sound of the well-remembered, old, cracked-voiced college-clock: it was comfortably near, yet not too near, Stoke Poges, where Gray was spending the summer with his mother and aunts.

Walpole could not settle anywhere without his baubles, his dogs and his cats. Patapan was no more, but two spaniels succeeded him, and two cats, Zara and Selima, formed part of the household and soon became as familiar to Gray as the backs of his friend's books and the colours of his china.

In February, 1747, a sad fate overtook one of them; she was, as later generations well know, 'drowned in a tub of goldfishes'. On learning of this disaster Gray wrote from Cambridge a letter too delightful not to be quoted almost in full:

> As one ought to be particularly careful to avoid blunders in a compliment of condolence, it would be a sensible satisfaction to me (before I testify my sorrow and the sincere part I take in your misfortune) to know for certain who it is I lament. I knew Zara and Selima, (Selima, was it, or Fatima?) or rather I knew them both together; for I cannot justly say which was which. Then as to your handsome Cat, the name you distinguish her by, I am no less at a loss, as well knowing one's handsome cat is always the cat one likes best; or, if one be alive and the other dead, it is usually the latter that is the handsomest.

Thomas Gray,
(1716-1771).

Oh, no! I would rather seem to mistake, and imagine to be sure it must be the tabby one that had met with this sad accident. Till this affair is a little better determined you will excuse me if I do not begin to cry.

He may not have begun to cry; but before he closed the letter he added the *Ode* on *feue Mademoiselle Selime* which would immortalize her not 'for one week or fortnight' as he modestly foretold, but for all time.

'Twas on a lofty vase's side
Where China's gayest art had dyed
 The azure flowers that blow;
Demurest of the tabby kind,
The pensive Selima reclined,
 Gazed on the lake below.

Her conscious tail her joy declared,
The fair round face, the snowy beard,
 The velvet of her paws,
Her coat, that with the tortoise vies,
Her ears of jet and emerald eyes,
 She saw; and purred applause.

Still had she gazed; but 'midst the tide
Two angel forms were seen to glide,
 The genii of the stream;
Their scaly armour's Tyrian hue
Through richest purple to the view
 Betrayed a golden gleam.

The hapless nymph with wonder saw;
A whisker first and then a claw
 With many an ardent wish
She stretched, in vain, to reach the prize.
What female heart can gold despise,
 What cat's averse to fish?

Presumptuous Maid! with looks intent,
Again she stretched, again she bent,
　　Nor knew the gulf between.
(Malignant Fate sat by and smiled)
The slippery verge her feet beguiled,
　　She tumbled headlong in.

Eight times emerging from the flood,
She mewed to every watery god
　　Some speedy aid to send.
No Dolphin came, no Nereid stirred,
No cruel Tom or Susan heard,
　　A Favourite has no friend.

From hence, ye Beauties, undeceived,
Know one false step is ne'er retrieved,
　　And be with caution bold.
Not all that tempts your wandering eyes
And heedless hearts is lawful prize,
　　Nor all that glistens gold.

Walpole was inordinately proud that his cat should have been lamented in so charming a poem by so admired a friend. After Gray's death he enthroned the 'lofty vase' on a pedestal at Strawberry Hill,[4] engraved with the first six lines of the *Ode*, only altering the first to

'Twas on this lofty vase's side.

In 1748 Dodsley included the *Ode* in the second volume of his *Collection of Poems*, but it appeared anonymously as 'By Mr——'. More than twenty years later Walpole was half-amused and half-annoyed to find in Shenstone's letters something which he did not know and which he believed Mr Gray himself never knew; namely that the Selima *Ode* was written to ridicule Lord Lyttelton's *Monody on the Death of his Lady*. 'It is just as true', he comments vehemently, 'as that the latter will survive and the former will be forgotten.' And as late as 1783 he still cherishes the vase, and the memory of the cat, and the echoes of the *Ode*. He then wrote to his cousin Field-Marshal Conway, whose charming wife, Lady Aylesbury, was collecting goldfish:

*Ode on the Death of a Favourite Cat*, design 4 by William Blake, the printed version.

I have taken out fifteen young fish of a year-and-a-half old—and have reserved them as an offering worthy of Amphitrite in the vase, the cat's vase, 'amidst the azure flowers that blow'.

But the most delightful tribute to be paid to the cat and her vase was when Dodsley published in March, 1758, a small folio of *Designs by Mr R. Bentley for Six Poems by Mr T. Gray*. Three years later Walpole and Bentley fell out, but when the illustrations to the *Odes* were produced the wayward and witty son of the famous Master of Trinity was still one of the most valued segments in the Strawberry Hill circle. That egregious shrew, Mrs Richard Bentley, had not then by her constant intrusions made more difficult the relations between the two men. Bentley's was a prickly character, and Walpole's was not without prickles of its own; but it should be remembered that twenty years later the lord of Strawberry Hill was giving secret financial assistance to his quondam crony, for the benefit of whose orphan children he placed a sum of money 'in the Funds'.

The sun was shining undimmed over the Gothic pinnacles at Twickenham when the designs for Gray's *Odes* were made. Bentley was an amateur; but his gay wit and light, flickering fancy atone for any technical imperfections, and three of the six *Odes* exactly suited his peculiar bent. These were the one on the distant prospect of Eton College, the Long Story, and—obviously—the Pensive Selima.

In this last the whimsy was what Walpole himself might have conceived—he may even have supplied some of the ideas. We see mourning cats in the horrible panoply of Augustan grief, black sashes round their hats, black scarves round their bodies; Fate cutting the ninefold threads of the proverbial lives; a company of mice exulting over the death of their foe; and finally Selima being ferried over the Styx by Charon, arching her back and spitting defiance at all three truculent heads of Cerberus.

In 1757 Walpole was writing to his charming friend, Lady Hervey, that if Lady Stafford will assist him in securing a picture and some letters of Ninon de l'Enclos he will add St Raoul to his calendar, Raoul being Lady Stafford's apparently much-cherished cat. In the matter of names for his own pets he presently deserted the oriental complexion of Zara and Selima to bestow the sturdy Anglo-Saxon cognomen of Harold on one beast which, having been rescued from shipwreck off the Goodwin Sands, was said to have attained the respectable age of fifteen years.

The fourth member of the group of Augustan cat-lovers was long remembered rather for his pitiful destiny and for the kindly tolerance

Martin Ferdinand Quadal, (1736-1811), cats with fish.

shown to him by Dr Johnson than for his quality as a poet. He was, in a sense, a one-poem man, His *Song of David*, not recovered in its entirety till well into the nineteenth century, has now been firmly established in an honourable niche, in spite of the circumstances and the place in which it was written, but his strange, rhapsodical, yet oddly moving *Jubilate Agno*, another work of the period of his mental eclipse, is mentioned neither in the 1913 edition of the sixteen-volume *Cambridge History of English Literature* nor in the 1944 *Oxford Companion*.

It has been left for sympathetic cat-lovers of a later vintage to rediscover his cat Jeffry, to call their own cats after him, and to range him with Lord Southampton as a prisoner of destiny whose solitude was relieved and his mind diverted by the presence of his purring friend. Friend, not servant, much less serf; there lies the fundamental difference between the two domestic pets who divide the heart of mankind in almost equal portions.

Jeffry, says Christopher Smart, is worthy to be presented before the throne of grace. 'I will', he announces, 'consider my cat Jeffry. For he is the servant of the living God and daily serving Him.'

He describes in detail how Jeffry, on rising in the morning, 'wreathes his body seven times round with elegant quickness', sharpens his claws, washes himself, looks up for instructions, goes off in quest of food. He propounds an original and surprising theory as to the motive behind the feline instinct to toy with a captive mouse. He sees no cruelty here at all, not even a sort of ferocious mischief.

> When he takes his prey he plays with it to give it a chance, for one mouse in seven escapes by his dallying.

Had Jeffry grown so stout during his sojourn within the Rules of the King's Bench that he lacked the activity needed to keep down this unusual average? His master would have rejected this idea: he took pride in what he called the 'briskness' of his companion. The words in which he sets down his impressions are wild and wandering enough, but the picture is instinct with life and shot through with poetry. Jeffry, he writes,

> keeps the Lord's watch in the night against the adversary—he counteracts the powers of darkness by his electrical skin and glaring eyes—in his morning orisons he loves the sun and the sun loves him.

We seem to be carried back in time to Montaigne's tower, or even as far as the world of Bartholomew the Englishman, though only one member of his Order, Roger Bacon to wit, might possibly have contemplated with a questioning, scientific eye the sparks that could be rubbed out of a cat's spine. It was by 'stroaking' Jeffry that Christopher Smart 'found out electricity'. He tells us that Jeffry

> has the subtlety and hissing of the serpent, which in goodness he suppresses. For he will not do destruction if he is well fed, neither will he spit without provocation. For he purrs with thankfulness when God tells him he is a good cat. For he is an instrument for the children to learn benevolence upon. For every house is incomplete without him and blessing is lacking in the spirit.

The English cats are the best in Europe, declares Smart: but it is upon one particular English cat that his wandering mind is focused. 'He is a mixture of gravity and waggery . . . there is nothing sweeter than his peace when he is at rest. There is nothing brisker than his life when he is in motion.' His tongue is 'exceeding pure', so that it possesses in purity what it lacks in music. Moreover, God had blest him with 'a variety of movements', so that, though he could not fly, he was 'an excellent clamberer'.

In the meantime English designers of pottery and porcelain were becoming conscious of the possible appeal of a kitten or a cat; witness the delectable Staffordshire kitten in the Victoria and Albert, with up-cocked blue-lined ears and a coat pranked with a delicate, fernlike pattern of the same colour.

6

# Some Augustan and
# Regency Cats

A conversation between Hodge, Selima and Jeffry might be well worth
overhearing. Hodge would boast of his master's dutiful attentions,
the oysters regularly supplied, the large expanse of waistcoat always
available as a place of repose: Selima, being a lady, might be more
inclined to praise the elegance of her surroundings, and the care with
which *her* particular human vassal kept himself crisply clean. With
Sophoclean irony, the unconscious and therefore the most devastating
kind, she would observe that *if* at any time she should desire *fresh* fish,
*really* fresh, some most unusual golden ones were kept for her delectation
in a lofty Chinese vase pranked with azure flowers.

But only Jeffry could claim that his master declared him worthy to be
presented before the throne of grace, and by 'stroking' his coat found
out the odd thing called 'electricity' that human beings were beginning
to speculate so much about.

What could William Cowper's cats contribute to the symposium?
Hodge and Jeffry might have bragged in the words of Montrose, 'As
Alexander I will reign, and I will reign alone': Selima had perforce to
share her master's affections with one other cat and at least two dogs;
but at Orchard Side, Olney, Cowper's cats were constrained to live on
terms of amity with three tame hares and a spaniel.

Low down in the hall door a little hatch had been made, that
these unusual inmates might come and go at their will. Yet what self-
respecting cat would believe that it was for them and not for her that
the thing had been planned and done? These Buckinghamshire cats
might well have maintained that no master was in himself a more

lovable man than theirs. But was he a dyed-in-grain cat-man? We shall see.

They certainly scored over Messrs Hodge and Jeffry and Madam Selima in one important point. A poem that was an epic and not an elegy had been composed in honour of certain of their number, ending, as an epic should, with the death of a formidable foe. This was *The Colubriad*. Another poem would be dedicated to an adventure which befell another of Cowper's cats. This was *The Retired Cat*. Yet each poem reveals a flaw in the poet's catmanity, a defect of which Johnson, Walpole or Smart would have been incapable.

The incident upon which *The Colubriad* was founded is related in a letter to the Rev. William Unwin, dated 3 August 1782.

Passing from the greenhouse into the barn I saw three kittens (we have so many in our retinue) looking with fixed attention at something which lay on the threshold of a door coiled up. I took but little notice of them at first but a loud hiss engaged me to attend more closely, when behold, a

The Rake's Progress, plate I, the Inheritance, 1735. An engraving after William Hogarth, (1697-1764). Note the scrawny and not very complimentary representation of the family cat.

viper! The largest I remember to have seen, rearing itself, darting its forked tongue and ejaculating the aforementioned hiss at the nose of a kitten almost in contact with his lips. I ran into the hall for a hoe with a long handle, with which I intended to assail him, and returning in a few seconds missed him: he was gone and I feared had escaped me. Still however the kitten sat watching immovably on the same spot. I concluded therefore that, sliding between the door and the threshold, he had found his way out of the garden into the yard. I went round immediately and there found him in close conversation with the old cat, whose curiosity being excited by so novel an appearance, inclined her to pat his head repeatedly with her fore-foot; with her claws however sheathed, and not in anger, but in the way of philosophical enquiry and examination.

To prevent her falling a victim to so laudable an exercise of her talents, I interposed in a moment with the hoe and performed upon him an act of decapitation which, though not immediately mortal, proved so in the end. Had he slid into the passages, where it is dark, or had he, when in the yard, met no interruption from the cat and secreted himself in one of the outhouses, it is hardly possible but that some of the family must have been bitten.

His first anxiety, before he had time to imagine the viper's stealthy escape into the dark passages or its invasion of the outhouses beyond, was lest the sinister visitant should deprive the household of their only cat 'that was of age to combat with a rat'. He dealt energetically with the crisis:

> With outstretched hoe I slew him at the door
> And taught him NEVER TO COME THERE NO MORE.

Yet it would have been his own fault if the episode had ended otherwise; for he had passed by the kittens 'taking little notice of them', not deeming them 'worth a poet's care'. Six years later, when he had bidden farewell to the bleak market-place of Olney and the long, tangled garden behind Orchard Side, he wrote to his charming cousin, Lady Hesketh, from his last Buckinghamshire home, Weston Lodge, a letter which reveals some responsiveness to the charm of the kitten kind but an implicit lack of enthusiasm for the ultimate and inevitable cat.

I have a kitten, my dear, the drollest of all creatures that ever wore a cat's skin. Her gambols are not to be described and would be incredible if they could. In point of size she is likely to be a kitten always, being extremely small of her age, but time, I suppose, that spoils everything, will make her a cat. You will see her, I hope, before that melancholy period shall arrive, for no wisdom that she may gain by experience and reflection hereafter will compensate the loss of her present hilarity.

She is dressed in a tortoise-shell suit and I know that you will delight in her.

It is curious that Cowper, who gave personal names to his spaniel and his three pet hares, should have left his cats and kittens anonymous. For all his playful tenderness there was something missing in his regard for his cats. This he unconsciously betrays in *The Retired Cat*, one of the last light-hearted trifles which he wrote before the final tempest wrecked his mind.

The poem begins with quite a pleasant little sketch of the character and habits of the anonymous animal. She was 'a poet's cat, sedate and grave'—

William Cowper, (1731-1800), a portrait by Lemuel Francis Abbott.

how different from the brisk and waggish Jeffry!—always in quest of some nook where she might repose or sit and think. Sometimes she would ascend an apple tree or a lofty pear, whence she liked to watch the gardener at his work. Sometimes she would curl herself up snugly in an old watering-pot:

> There wanting nothing but a fan
> To seem some nymph in her sedan.

But up the tree she was too much exposed to the wind; the watering-pot was 'cold and comfortless within'; so she betook herself to her master's bedroom to seek 'some place of more serene repose'.

> A drawer—it chanced at bottom lined
> With linen of the softest kind
> A drawer impending o'er the rest
> Half-open in the topmost chest,[1]
> Of depth enough and none to spare
> Invited her to slumber there.
> Puss with delight beyond expression
> Surveyed the scene and took possession.

Lulled by her own purring she left the cares of life behind and slumbered fast and long. Then in came Susan the housemaid and

> By no malignity impelled,
> But all unconscious what it held,

shut the drawer.

Puss was indignant at being roused, but confident that Susan would come at supper-time and let her out, she resigned herself to rest among the folded kerchiefs whose softness and sweetness made the place 'a delicate retreat'.

But Susan failed to return. Apparently Cowper did not seek a clean kerchief for forty-eight hours, for Puss remained entombed for that time, and nobody seems to have noticed her absence or to have heard the faint scratches and mews with which she tried to attract attention, till the poet in the middle of the second night became conscious of

> something imprisoned in the chest.

Doubtful as to what the 'something' might be, he 'resolved it should continue there'; but fortunately

> —a voice which well he knew,
> A long and melancholy mew,
> Saluting his poetic ears
> Consoled him and dispelled his fears.

He left his bed, and, following the universal rule, he started his hunt in the bottom drawer instead of in the top.

> Forth skipped the cat; not now replete
> As erst with airy self conceit
> Nor in her own fond apprehension
> A theme for all the world's attention,
> But modest, sober, cured of all
> Her notions hyperbolical.

It is not difficult to imagine what a true lover of cats would have done next. Slippered and night-capped, candle in hand, he would have raided the larder in quest of fish and milk to restore the languishing captive. Cowper may have done this; one hopes that he *did*. But all he tells us is that, having liberated the cat, he went back to bed.

Greater sensibility would have been shown by Mrs Tofts, the eccentric opera singer of the late eighteenth century, who left legacies to her twenty cats and seems to have felt the wrench of parting from them more acutely than any other pang. As Peter Pindar put it:

> Not Niobe mourned more for fourteen brats,
> Not Mrs Tofts to leave her twenty cats.

In the same year that Cowper's cats had their memorable encounter with the viper there was born at the Château of La Rivière, on the banks of the Dordogne, a boy whose infant resemblance to a kitten came near costing him his life. This was Marcellin de Marbot, later to blossom into a Colonel of the 3rd Mounted Chasseurs and a General in Napoleon's *Grande Armée*. As he had a rather upturned nose and a round face, his father nicknamed him *le petit chat*. In his own words, 'nothing more was necessary to make so young a child wish to play at being a cat'.

The family cat gets into the nursery scene. Jean-Honoré Fragonard, The Visit to the Nursery, *c.* 1775.

Jean-Baptiste Greuze, The Wool Winder, *c.* 1759.
*The Frick Collection*

It was his greatest delight to crawl about on all fours, mewing vigorously. Every day he used to clamber up to the second floor of the Château and invade the library where it was his father's habit to take refuge during the hottest hours of summer. As soon as he heard the mewing of his *petit chat* the elder Marbot would open the door. Then, after giving the young visitor an illustrated volume of Buffon's *Histoire Naturelle* with which to amuse himself, he would plunge again into his own studies. These occasions were the joy of little Marcellin; but on one memorable day he failed to gain admission by his first tentative *miaow*. Papa, deep in more serious matters, did not hear the voice of his *petit chat* and consequently did not fling wide the door. In vain was the mewing repeated in the most appealing tone; the door remained inflexibly shut.

Presently Marcellin's eyes fell upon the little opening known as a *chatière*, found in all the châteaux of southern France and placed at floor-level for the benefit of the family cat. This was obviously his own special means of entry. He promptly stretched himself flat on the parquet; and a moment later the head of *le petit chat* had been thrust through the *chatière*. But where the head went the body could not follow; when he tried to retreat, he realized that he was trapped. Yet even in that predicament he would not call for help in his own natural and recognizable voice. At all costs he must continue to play his self-appointed role of a little cat. He played it so well, and made noises so like those of an agitated *minet* that Papa, imagining the whole thing to be a joke, was seized with inextinguishable laughter.

Presently the mewing grew fainter, the round, snub-nosed face turned blue, and *le petit chat* lost consciousness. 'Imagine my father's concern', wrote Marbot many years later, 'when at last he realized what was happening!' Not without difficulty the door was heaved off its hinges and the unfortunate child extricated. Papa bore him off to Mama, who, thinking that he was dead, had hysterics on the spot.

When Marcellin came to himself a surgeon was in the act of bleeding him. The sight of the blood and of the anxious faces bending over him impressed the scene so strongly on his memory that it was still vivid when his *Mémoires* were written more than fifty years later.

Joseph Nollekens, the notoriously avaricious sculptor, kept a cat, who must have been an expert mouser to sustain life in that meagre Mortimer Street house where it was Lent all the year round. A master who would plank down an annual guinea to get an opportunity to filch nutmegs from the Royal Academy banquet could hardly be expected to lay out even

Jean Baptiste Antoine Marcellin Marbot, (1782-1854).

a few grudging pence with the itinerant cat's-meat man, much less with the fishmonger or the smock-frocked milkmonger with his great wooden yoke over his shoulders and his clashing cans on either hand. Yet even he cared sufficiently for his cat to give her a name—Jenny Dawdle: and when he and his dusky-complexioned maid of all work, Elizabeth Rosina Clements, otherwise 'Black Bet', were well stricken in years old Harpagon liked to see her dancing Jenny Dawdle round the studio, watched by the inexpressive eyes of half-finished busts and statues and stirring up drifts of marble dust as they danced. They were also watched by the amused eyes of Nolleken's pupils, one of whom, J. T. Smith, wrote his life and incidentally immortalized his dark-skinned Abigail and his dancing cat.

*Willie's Wife* in Robert Burns's satirical poem of that name must have closely resembled 'Black Bet', whose looks were ascribed to one—or both—of two causes; a strain of negro blood or a complete dearth of soap in the meagre household at Mortimer Street. We meet the name 'Bawdrins' again after an interval of more than two centuries, but this time it is borne by a female cat.

> Auld Bawdrins by the ingle sits
> And wi' her loof her face is washin';
> But Willie's wife is nae sae trig
>   She dichts her grunsy wi' a hashin'.

Which is as much as to say that while Bawdrins washed her face with her paw, Mrs Willie, less dainty, dabbed hers with a stocking. How ineffective the dabbing process proved is indicated by the remark that

> Her face wad fyle the Logan water.

Walter Scott, like Horace Walpole, was able to find a place in his capacious heart for cats as well as dogs; and, indeed, for pigs and hens as well as donkeys. The cat who was his constant companion at his house in North Castle Street, Edinburgh, was named Hinse of Hinsfeldt, after the hero of a German fairy-tale. Lockhart gives us a vivid glimpse of the small, square room to the rear of the dining-parlour which was Scott's library, workshop and place of refuge from 1798 to 1826. He describes the walls lined with books, old and new, the massy writing-table, the solitary picture, a portrait of Graham of Claverhouse, over the mantelpiece with a Highland target on either side and broadswords and dirks 'dispersed star-fashion around them'.

The noble Maida, couchant on the hearth-rug, waited for a snap of his master's fingers to rise and lay his head upon his knee. From the top of 'a sort of ladder, low, broad, well-carpeted, and strongly guarded with oaken rails', they were solemnly watched by Hinse of Hinsfeldt. Lockhart remembered Hinse as 'venerable, fat and sleek, and no longer very locomotive', but it was said that in his younger days he had been well able to hold his own against the 'Shirra's' many dogs. Now he preferred the dignified security of the top step, whence he would not stir till Maida thumped on the door with his huge paw as a signal that he wished to be let out;

> and then Hinse came down purring from his perch and mounted guard by the footstool, *vice* Maida absent on furlough.

In the course of his travels in Italy during the last year of his life, Scott visited the Bishop of Tarentum, and noted in his Journal that he found in him 'a total absence of that rigid stiffness which hardens the hearts of the old and converts them into a sort of petrifaction'. The next sentence perhaps gives the clue to that engaging youthfulness of mind.

> Apparently his foible was a fondness for cats. One of them, a superb brindled Persian, is a great beauty and seems a particular favourite. . . . I once saw at Lord Yarmouth's house a Persian cat but not quite so fine as that of the Bishop.

'Yarmouth Bloaters', otherwise 'Lord Monmouth', otherwise 'Lord Steyne', was, then, another lover of cats. Curious that in the complex character of such a reprobate there should have been room for two

Sir Walter Scott, (1771-1832), a portrait by Sir Henry Raeburn.

Sir Walter Scott's Cat
*Hinse of Hinsefeldt* in
the Armoury.

perfectly innocent 'foibles'—the giants on the clock outside St Dunstan's in the West (a life-long delight); and a Persian cat, even if not so fine a cat as the Bishop of Tarentum's.

There seems to be little doubt that this Bishop was identical with the 'good old Cardinal . . .' with whom Samuel Rogers used to dine 'very often' during his sojourn in Italy more than ten years earlier. He also dined with the Cardinal's cats; for they always sat at his table and were much the gravest of the company. One is irresistibly reminded of Archbishop Laud and his parti-coloured pets.

It is a long step from the Augustan technique, the heroic couplets, the desiccated symmetry of Rogers and the warmer, wider, more flexible mentality of the poets who were the glory of the Romantic heyday. Southey was, no doubt, the least inspiring and the least inspired of the group; but he of them all was the prime cat-lover. It was he who said that 'a kitten was in the animal world what a rosebud is in a garden'. He himself owned a whole succession of cats, ending with an individual named Hurlyburlybuss—surely a coinage of one of the Southey children, that? In his poem, *The Witch*, a farmer thus describes the village sybil:

> —She sits there, nose to knees,
> Smoke-dried and shrivelled o'er a starvèd fire,
> With that black cat beside her, whose great eyes
> Shine like Beelzebub's, and to be sure
> It must be one of his imps.

The Farmer's son wants to know

> What makes her sit there moping by herself
> With no soul near her but that great black cat?

It was indeed fortunate for her that Matthew Hopkins was not there to give the answer.

The *Comic Annual* seems an unlikely place in which to find a sonnet by Keats, yet it printed one within nine years of his death, a trifle dating from 1818, when it was written in honour of the family cat at the house in Lamb's Conduit Street occupied by the Reynolds family. He was an elderly, asthmatic cat, lacking the tip of his tail, and in his day a 'bonny fechter'. Keats thus apostrophizes him:

Cat! who hast passed thy grand climacteric,
How many mice and rats hast in thy days
Destroyed? How many titbits stolen? Gaze
With those bright, languid segments green, and prick
Those velvet ears, but prith'ee do not stick
Thy latent talons in me—but upraise
Thy gentle mew and tell me all thy frays
Of fish and mice and rats and tender chick.

The 'latent talons' had apparently been stuck into the poet's hand or knee on at least one occasion; but he was merciable. He saw the beauty of the old hero's green eyes and velvet ears, and it must have been by stroking him that he discovered that his fur was still as soft as when in his youth he had entered the lists upon 'glass-bottled wall'.

Three months later he was writing to John Reynolds, his particular friend in that family, a wild whimsy upon the 'things all disjointed' that came before his eyes as he lay in bed. They are fantastic enough, these visions; Voltaire in medieval armour, Alexander with his nightcap on,

Old Socrates a-tying his cravat
And Hazlitt playing with Miss Edgeworth's cat.

*The Cat's Lunch*, a
nineteenth-century painting
by Marguerite Gérard.

The essence of the absurdity would seem to lie in the admittedly savage character of the great critic ('your only good damper') contrasted with the gentle and playful occupation in which he is engaged.

That curious fragment, *The Eve of St Mark*, contains, among other anticipations of William Morris in mock-medieval mood, a description of a 'warm-angled winter screen' painted with 'many monsters', Siamese doves, Peruvian mice, birds of paradise, 'macaw and tender avadavat';

> And silken-furred Angora Cat.

Keats must surely have seen just such a screen in the house of one of his friends. It sounds the sort of thing that might have stood in Leigh Hunt's Hampstead villa. The Angora cat is, however, in unexpected company and, if the creatures on the screen had come to life, would have 'wrought a sair havoc' among them, as the Scottish Minister said that Absolom had wrought 'among the lassies of Jerusalem'.

A living cat formed one of the circle in several of the families most visited by Keats during the last years of his life. The wife of Charles Wentworth Dilke had two, concerning whom John inserted a gay passage in a long, not uniformly gay letter to his brother George and sister-in-law Georgina (née Wylie) after their departure to the American backwoods in the summer of 1818, and after the death of their young brother Tom at the end of the same year.

Keats felt the loss of Tom with all the passion of his passionate nature; but a sort of irresponsible gaiety often breaks in upon normal sorrow, especially when the source lies in some recent event. At Wentworth Place, with the Dilkes next door to him, indeed, under the same roof, Keats, though under the double strain of grieving for Tom and falling in love with Fanny Brawne, could jest about Mrs Dilke's cats in his old, staccato style.

> Mrs Dilke has two Cats—a Mother and a Daughter now the Mother is a tabby and the daughter a black and white like the spotted child— Now it appears quite ominous to me, for the doors of both houses are opened frequently—so that there is a complete thoroughfare for both Cats (there being no board up to the contrary) they may one and several of them come into my room *ad libitum*. But no—the Tabby only comes—whether from Sympathy from Ann the Maid or

*Above left:* *The Country Wedding* by John Lewis Krimmel, 1820. Note the cat at the top of the cabinet.

*Above right:* A rural scene from the low countries. *Harris Museum & Art Gallery*

*A Young Boy Playing with a Cat*, John Opie, (1761-1807).

me I cannot tell. The Cat is not an old Maid herself—her daughter is a proof of it. I have questioned her—I have looked at the lines of her paw—I have felt her pulse—to no purpose. Why should the old Cat come to me? I ask myself—and myself has not a word to answer.

The answer might well lie in the presence next door of Charles Wentworth Dilke Junior, a lively eight-year-old whose instinctive teasing the black-and-white daughter might find it easier to endure—or even to elude—than her tabby mother.

George Keats was in England again in January, 1820, and in a letter written to Georgina soon after her husband's arrival, to be delivered by him on his almost precipitate return, John makes an allusion to her mother's 'quaker-coloured cat' which surely ought not to be taken too seriously. There had been 'a fine packing up' at the Wylie's house prior to George's departure. 'Thinking you might want a Rat-catcher', wrote Keats, 'I put your mother's old quaker-coloured cat into the top of your bonnet—she's wi' kitten, so you may expect to find a whole family—I hope the family will not grow too large for its lodging.' Was George really expected to open the bonnet-box and feed the quaker-coloured cat during the voyage to America? Against the apparent insensibility of this jest—for jest it must have been—we may set the picture of John Keats as described by his friend Charles Cowden Clarke in the story of a pugilistic encounter with a Hampstead butcher-boy. The brute, said Keats, was tormenting a kitten, and he interfered, when a 'threat offered was enough for his mettle', and they 'set to'.

> He thought he should be beaten, for the fellow was the taller and stronger; but like an authentic pugilist my young poet found that he had planted a blow which 'told' upon his antagonist: in every succeeding round therefore (for they fought nearly an hour) he never failed of returning to this weak point, and the contest ended in the hulk being led home.

Shelley also was capable of using his fists upon 'brutes' of the same order, but while Keats's cats, even the Angora on the 'warm-angled winter screen', are credible, natural creatures, there is a touch of fantasy in the allusion which occurs in the older poet's diary under the date 6 October 1818.

John Keats, (1795-1821), a portrait by William Hilton.

On this day Mary put her head through the door and said, 'Come and look: here's a cat eating roses; she'll turn into a woman. When beasts eat these roses they turn into men and women.'

Mrs Shelley might well have found in that sight the germ of a creepy story quite as weird as *Frankenstein* but rather less gruesome.

A cat sat in reverence before the grave of John Keats in the Protestant Cemetery, Rome.

7

# A Few Victorian and Post-Victorian Cats

The Cat's-meat man (whom presumably Joseph Nollekens, RA, did not patronize) was one of the familiar figures in the teeming London streets during the first half of the nineteenth century. 'Vy, sir,' said one of the dealers to Henry Mayhew, 'can you tell me 'ow many people's in London?' 'Upwards of two millions,' was the reply. 'I don't know nothing vatever about millions,' said the cat's-meat man, 'but I think there's a cat to every ten people, so you can reckon.'

He added that he 'sarved' about two hundred cats, some of whom had a 'hap'orth' of meat a day, or every other day. Times being bad, few owners could afford a daily 'penn'orth'. It was, of course, horse-meat, collected from the knacker's yards and sold at the rate of 2½d a pound or, in small pieces on skewers, at a farthing, a halfpenny, or a penny each.

A motorized age finds it difficult to realize the number of mews and stables then scattered about London, from the tumbledown shed sheltering the costermonger's donkey to the spacious stalls, and loose-boxes, and coach-houses at the rear of the great houses in the West End. Where there were horses there would be a cat. The coachmen in the mews at the back of the squares were very good customers, said Mayhew's informant. Old maids, on the other hand, were 'bad, though very plentiful' patrons of the trade. It was their regrettable habit to cheapen the wares till the unfortunate seller could 'scarcely live at the business'.

Even if the cats of the neighbourhood had not recognized his little cart with its gruesome load, the cat's-meat man would have been known for what he was, whether at the receipt of custom or otherwise. He wore 'a shiny hat, black plush waistcoat and sleeves, a blue apron, corduroy trousers, and a blue and white spotted handkerchief round the neck'. The more sparkish among them would wear two or three of these handkerchiefs, after the manner of old Mr Brontë with his multiple stocks.

There was at least one spinster in Early Victorian London who was a lavish patroness. This was a lady of colour who would buy as much as one shilling and fourpence-worth of cat's meat a day, climb up on to the roof of her house, and feed 'the cats on the tiles'. She insisted that her daily supply should be brought to her before ten o'clock in the morning: if it did not arrive, she sent to the shop for it. One can well believe that between ten and eleven o'clock the 'noise and cries of the hundreds of strays attracted to the spot' were so terrible to hear that 'the parties in the vicinity complained'.

It will be remembered that among the extensive and peculiar acquaintances of Sam Weller was a pieman who 'could make pies out of anything'.

'What a number o' cats you keep, Mr Brooks,' says I, when I'd got intimate with him. 'Ah,' says he, 'I do—a good many,' says he. 'You must be very fond of cats,' says I. 'Other people is,' says he, winkin' at me—'Why, what do you mean?' says I. 'Mean?' says he. 'That I'll never be a party to the combination o' the butchers to keep up the prices o' meat,' says he. 'Mr Weller,' says he, squeezing my hand very hard and vispering in my ear, 'don't mention this again, but it's the seasonin' as does it. They're all made o' them noble animals,' says he, a-pointin' to a very nice little tabby kitten, 'I seasons 'em for beefsteak, weal or kidney, 'cordin to the demand.'

It is hardly surprising that after hearing some further instances of the pieman's skill in his craft Mr Pickwick should have remarked 'with a slight shudder' that Sam's former acquaintance must have been 'a very ingenious young man'.

With relief we find that Henry Mayhew states categorically that the pies sold in the London Streets were 'made of beef or mutton'. Sam's horrific legend may have been current fourteen years earlier, but it had not reached Mayhew's ears when he was collecting the materials for his great survey, and he was certainly not too squeamish to allude to it if it had.

Dickens gives us one of the last glimpses of a cat in the guise of a witch's familiar. This was the old black cat belonging to that notorious child-queller, Mrs Pipchin, she to whose 'infantine boarding-house' at Brighton Paul Dombey was sent for the benefit of sea-air. This cat

> generally lay coiled up upon the centre foot of the fender, purring egotistically and winking at the fire until the contracted pupils of his eyes were like two notes of admiration. The good old lady might have been—not to record it disrespectfully—a witch and Paul and the cat her two familiars, as they all sat by the fire together. It would have been quite in keeping with the appearance of the party if they had all sprung up the chimney in a high wind one night and never been heard of any more.

'This, however,' adds Dickens gravely, 'never came to pass.' The original of Mrs Pipchin was 'a reduced old lady' named Mrs Roylance with whom the very youthful Charles lodged for a time in Camden Town while his family were parked in the Marshalsea and he himself was working in the rat-infested warehouse by Hungerford Stairs, pasting wrappings and labels on Warren's blacking. Mrs Roylance's dreary little dwelling can have borne little resemblance to the 'ogress's castle' at Brighton, nor was her 'infantine boarding-house' conducted upon what Mrs Chick described as 'an exceedingly limited and particular scale'; but knowing the keen eye for detail already possessed by at least one of her forlorn little boarders we may feel quite certain that she had a cat, and a black one, too.

At Dover Miss Betsy Trotwood had, when her nephew David Copperfield startled her by his sudden appearance, one cat and two canaries. All these pets were still in being when she and Mr Dick turned up so unexpectedly at David's lodgings in Buckingham Street, Strand, where, to his amazement, he found his aunt 'sitting on a quantity of luggage with her two birds before her and her cat on her knee, like a female Robinson Crusoe, drinking tea'.

A lank and meagre cat shared with the equally lank and meagre Marchioness the cellar in Bevis Marks where Dick Swiveller began his transformation from a shabby, cheeky young clerk into the most delightful, fantastic fellow in the world; but when we consider these cats we may be led to the conclusion that Dickens, even if he did not suffer a physical revulsion, was slightly antipathetic to the cat family in general.

Mrs Pipchin and her Familiar, from Hablot K. Browne's illustration to *Dombey and Son*, 1847.

*Above left:* George Cruikshank's Mr Pickwick with a cat at his foot and a cat on the mantelpiece.

*Above right:* George Cruikshank's Mr Bumble and Mrs Corney taking tea.

Might not Mercutio with some reason have apostrophized Mr Carker the Manager as 'Prince of Cats'?

It was otherwise with Thackeray, whose favourite, Louisa, was as fond of reclining on his waistcoat as Hodge was of reclining on Dr Johnson's. He fed her, not with oysters, but with fish from his own plate at breakfast; and when her company became irksome he would 'take her up very gently and put her outside the door'. She must have been the 'little cat passionately attached to Papa' of whom his elder daughter Anny was writing to Mrs Baxter in October 1861.

By that time the Thackerays had quitted the squat, bow-fronted house in Young Street, Kensington, where *Vanity Fair* was written; but both Anny and Minny cherished memories of 'the bit of garden with the medlar tree' where Minny was wont to assemble her large family of adopted strays and to feed them from little saucers placed in a row along the terrace beneath Papa's study window. She named them after characters in Dickens's novels. Nicholas Nickleby was 'a huge grey tabby' and Barnaby Rudge, appropriately enough, the weakling of the company.

Two imaginary yet famous small girls of the Victorian or Crinoline Period possessed pet cats: Dr Hoffmann's Paulinchen in Germany and Lewis Carroll's Alice in England. Paulinchen was re-christened by the resourceful lady[5] who translated *Strutwelpeter* into English, and given the name of Harriet as more likely to appeal to young readers in this country. Without in the least underrating the virtues of the translation, I confess that I have lately found much pleasure in the original text introduced to me by a friend. The illustrations are, of course, identical. One sees Minz and Maunz in both, playing the part of *strophe* and *antistrophe* in a Greek play as the tragedy unfolds itself.

When Paulinchen, left alone in the house, goes prancing gaily towards the chest of drawers where the large matchbox stands, each cat raises a minatory paw. When a match is struck, both paws are uplifted in protest, and two pairs of jaws part to let out an anxious *Miau! Mio!* They remind the disobedient child that her father had forbidden this; but she pays no need. The match flickers and crackles merrily; Paulinchen, in her voluminous green frock, jumps as merrily to and fro.

Minz and Maunz raise their paws higher and open their jaws wider. Mother also had forbidden this thing. Let Paulinchen throw the match away, or she will soon be in a blaze. And when their prophecy is fulfilled, they cry aloud for help, squatting on their haunches, jaws agape, paws flung up and spread wide.

Minz and Maunz admonish Paulinchen from Dr Hoffmann's *Struwelpeter*, 1847.

At last only a gruesome mound of ashes remains, with a single small patch still smouldering and a plume of smoke rising like the cloud over a volcano. Poor little Minz and Maunz! They sit and weep, using yellow handkerchiefs to staunch the rush of tears from their eyes. In some mysterious manner a large bow of black crape has appeared on each tail. The English version says:

> Their tears ran down their cheeks so fast
> They made a little pool at last.

In the German version it is a little brook (*Bächlein*)not a pool. Flowing towards the spectator from two sides, its waters form a confluence in the centre of the scene, leaving the 'little scarlet shoes' pointing right and left in a heart-shaped patch of dry ground.

Lewis Carroll seems to have felt that no home which contained a small girl would be adequately furnished without a cat or kitten. The earlier Alice, she who was whisked off to a Wonderland where she met the characters from a pack of cards, had a cat called Dinah, of whom she thought even when she was falling down the rabbit-hole.

Dinah'll miss me very much tonight, I should think. I hope they'll remember her saucer of milk at tea-time. Dinah my dear, I wish you were down here with me!

And it may have been devotion to Dinah rather than disregard for a mouse's feelings when, having met one swimming in the Pool of Tears, she addressed to him the first question in her French lesson-book, namely, '*Où est ma chatte?*' Worse still, she went on to relate the merits of Dinah, a 'dear, quiet thing', who sat 'purring so nicely by the fire, licking her paws and washing her face', and was 'such a capital one for catching mice'. 'Our family', the quivering mouse told her, 'always *hated* cats; nasty, low vulgar things.'

Those who recognize the Alice books for the satirical *fabliaux* that they essentially are, feel no surprise at the large number of talking animals encountered there. The Cheshire Cat,[3] already preserved in a proverb, put on immortality when it appeared by the kitchen fire of the Ugly Duchess and later upon the bough of a tree above Alice's head.

By the time that Alice climbed through the Looking Glass into a very strange game of chess Dinah was a respectable matron, the mother of a black kitten and a white one. When the story opens the white kitten is being strenuously cleaned by its mother and the black one is 'having a grand game of romps with the ball of worsted Alice had been trying to wind up'. On waking from her dream the little girl has a confused idea that the black kitten must have been the Red Queen and its sister 'her White Majesty'. How brief a space of time the whole adventure lasted may be judged from the fact that when Alice slowly struggled back to consciousness Dinah was still busy about the white kitten's toilet.

'Now, Kitty, let's consider who it was that dreamed it all—you see, Kitty, it must have been either me or the Red King'—but Alice had already remarked upon the 'very inconvenient habit of kittens that, whatever you say to them, they always purr'. The kitten and the Rev. Charles Lutwidge Dodgson leave the problem for ever unsolved.

Harriet Martineau in the *Guides to Service* (1838-39) firmly informs the would-be Abigail that she will find that she has 'few pleasures'.

Your Sunday walk, a holiday now and then, an entertaining book and an hour to read it in, and perhaps a bird, a favourite plant or a kitten— these are nearly all your indulgences.

*Above left:* The Cheshire cat from Lewis Carroll's *Alice's Adventures in Wonderland*, 1865, illustrated by Sir John Tenniel, (1820-1914).

*Above right:* Alice with Dinah's black kitten.

Dinah's black kitten, from *Through the Looking Glass*.

One hopes that the kitten did not cease to be regarded as an 'indulgence' when it grew into a cat.

No doubt many maidservants took Miss Martineau as their oracle, but Mrs Carlyle's Helen Mitchell was not of their number. She thought poorly of 'Miss Martno': and on one occasion at least the domestic cat at Cheyne Row, far from being regarded as a mitigation of her lot, had a narrow escape from her wrath.

Weary of the unrelieved menu of roast mutton, hot or cold, which was the sea-mark of Mrs Carlyle's culinary sail, Helen petitioned for a red herring, and the petition was granted. Her mistress, hearing the parlour fire being relighted with 'a perfectly unexampled vengeance' and the tea-tray being clanked on the lobby table as if Helen 'were minded to demolish the whole concern at one fell stroke', conjectured that the red herring had disagreed with her. Geraldine Jewsbury, that oddest of literary ladies, who happened to be on a visit to the Carlyles, rather officiously descended to the kitchen to find the cause of the trouble. The first thing she noticed was the absence of a familiar object. 'Where,' she asked, 'is the cat?' 'The cat!—I have all but killed her.' 'How?' enquired the naturally startled Miss Jewsbury. 'With the besom.' 'Why, for goodness sake?' 'Why?' repeated Helen in fury. *Why* indeed? Because she ate my red herring. I set it all ready on the end of the dresser, and she ran away with it and ate it, every morsel, to the tail.' 'And have you had no dinner?' 'Oh, yes—I had mutton enough; but I had just set my heart on a red herring.'

The Cheyne Row cat had been privileged to see many of the eminent men who visited her master, Ruskin, Mazzini, Count d'Orsay, John Stuart Mill and Sir Henry Taylor among them, but it is probable that the one who cast upon her the most kindly glance was the 'fine, large-featured, dim-eyed, shaggy-headed' Alfred Tennyson, who spent many hours in the back-garden smoking 'infinite tobacco' with the sage.

In the *Idylls of the King*[4] Sir Gawain informs Sir Percivale that he will thenceforth 'be deafer than a blue-eyed cat'. Darwin in the *Origin of Species* had already remarked that 'cats which are entirely white and have blue eyes are generally deaf'; but it seems probable that Tennyson was an attentive cat-observer in his own right. It is curious that he should have omitted the mysterious cat from his verse-rendering of the *Voyage of Maelduin*; but he used a different and more didactic source.

*The Spinster's Sweet-Arts* is far from being the best of his Lincolnshire dialect pieces, but the soliloquy of the wise virgin who rejected all her wooers and kept her 'two 'oondred a-year' to herself shows that the poet was familiar with most aspects of cat-psychology. Her four cats it had pleased her to name after the four rejected suitors of her youth: 'Tommy the fust, an' Tommy the second, an' Steevie an' Rob.' The last had clearly come nearest to securing the prize:

> Naay—let ma stroäk tha down till I maäkes tha es smooth es silk,
> But ef I'ed married tha, Robby, thou'd not 'a been worth tha milk,
> Thou'd niver 'a cotch'd ony mice, but 'a left me the work to do,
>     And ta'en to the bottle beside, so es all that I 'ears be true;
> But I loovs tha to maäke thysen 'appy and soä purr awaäy, my dear,
> Thou'ed wellnigh purred me awaäy for' my oän two 'oondred-a-year.

The traditional association between the elderly lady and the cat is charmingly perpetuated in *Cranford*. Mrs Forrester was one of the few members of that exclusive circle of elderly ladies who had entered the honourable estate of matrimony, graduating thence to the dignified estate of widowhood, and, strangely enough, she is the only one of whom it is recorded that she kept a cat.

Concerning this animal she related an anecdote to another widow, Lady Glenmire, who had been admiring her very fine lace collar. 'I always wash it myself,' said Mrs Forrester. She had a very good receipt for washing it in milk, for, of course, such lace should never be starched or ironed.

> Well, ma'am, I had tacked it together—and put it to soak in milk, when unfortunately I left the room; on my return I found Pussy on the table, looking very like a thief, but gulping very uncomfortably. And would you believe it? At first I said 'Poor Pussy, poor Pussy!' till all at once I looked and saw the cup of milk—cleaned out! I believe I was provoked enough to give her a slap, which did no good but only helped the lace down . . .
>
> I could have cried, I was so vexed; but I determined I would not give the lace up without a struggle for it. I hoped the lace might disagree with her, at any rate; but it would have been too much for Job if he had seen, as I did, the cat come in, quite placid and purring not quarter of an hour after, and almost expecting to be stroked. 'No, Pussy,' said I, 'if you have any conscience you ought not to expect *that*.'

But a thought struck the indomitable lady. She despatched her little maid to the house of the local doctor, Mr Hoggins, with a polite request

for the loan of his top-boots for an hour. When the request, to the
accompaniment of much laughter from 'the young men in the surgery',
was duly granted, Mrs Forrester and her Abigail put Pussy into the top-
boot 'with her forefeet straight down so that she could not scratch' and
gave her a tartar emetic guilefully mixed with red-currant jelly. 'I shall
never forget,' related the old lady,

> how anxious I was for the next half hour. I took Pussy to my room,
> and spread a clean towel on the floor. I could have kissed her when she
> returned the lace to sight very much as it had gone down. Jenny had
> boiling water ready, and we soaked it and soaked it, and spread it on a
> lavender-bush in the garden before I could touch it again, even to put
> it in milk. But now your ladyship would never guess that it had been in
> pussy's inside.

Neither Mrs Gaskell nor Mrs Forrester pauses to explain how the lace
escaped being stained with the red-currant jelly.

A very small girl of the Alice period once went to visit a remarkable
kinswoman of hers at a house in Hampstead. This was one of the Clough
children, and her hostess was none other than Miss Nightingale, who
thus describes the scene in her bedroom during the visit.

> It came in its flannel coat to see me. No one had ever prepared me
> for its Royalty. It sat quite upright but would not say a word, good
> or bad. The cats jumped up, on which it put out its hand with a kind
> of gracious dignity and caressed them, as if they had been presenting
> Addresses, and they responded in a humble, grateful way, quite cowed
> by infant majesty.

It was in the same year that her father, employing every wile to lure
her back to her old home and to him, tried to soften her resistance by
describing the doings of the favourite cats she had left behind. A year
later, when she was in some distress of mind though not an inch nearer
to surrender, one of her Hampstead cats would kiss her eyelids and lick
the tears off her cheeks. And more than thirty years later she made this
characteristic avowal:

> I learn the lesson of life from a little kitten of mine, one of two. The old
> cat comes in and says, very cross, 'I didn't ask you in here. I like to have

my Missis to myself.' The bigger and handsomer kitten runs away; but the little one *stands her ground*: and when the old enemy comes near enough kisses his nose and makes the peace. That is the lesson of life; to kiss one's enemy's nose always standing one's ground.

Some eminent persons whom fate brought into close contact with Miss Nightingale may have been left in uncertainty as to whether it was a kiss or a scratch which she implanted upon their noses.

'Beware', said Voltaire once, 'of a woman who does not like cats.' In one respect at least two Eminent Victorians of the feminine gender would have met with his approval: Florence Nightingale and Christina Rossetti.

'The Jael,' as Swinburne called her, 'who led the Pre-Raphaelite hosts to victory', was a lover of animals all her life, particularly if they were small and soft. The oddly-assorted collection which Dante Gabriel assembled in his Chelsea garden was never too odd to appeal to her, though some of them, such as the 'wombat obtuse and furry', seem to have suggested the fantastic train of demi-beasts in *Goblin Market*. One of those creatures is described as having a cat's face and purring like a

Christina Rossetti,
September 1866.

cat. In *Sing-Song* she points out that 'a sailor's cat is not a cat', just as 'a soldier's frog is not a frog'. Her nursery-rhyme Pussy has 'a whiskered face' and 'such pretty ways', and puns on the rug: in *An Alphabet*

C is a Cat with a comical look.

Then, when we come to the last phase, when the rich Pre-Raphaelite colours have faded and her poems move into a world of delicate monochrome, we find her enjoying the company of a real cat and a real kitten in her dim drawing-room in Torrington Square, Bloomsbury. Little more than a year before her death she was writing to her surviving brother, the selfless if unorthodox William Michael:

I have turned doctor myself! Rubbing a kitten who appears weak, to say the least of it, in the hindlegs with camphorated oil. Yesterday I flattered myself that the treatment gave some promise of amendment. Such a pretty kitten, with such a rich fur: and it stood up yesterday at the fender and made the Y of our childhood.

Her admirer, Swinburne, apostrophized his particular cat as 'stately, kindly, lordly friend', and characteristically speaks of his own 'reverent hand's caress'; but it may be doubted whether any cat-lover of the late Victorian period ever allowed the dear creatures to pervade his nights and days as did the painter, Albert Moore. Graham Robertson, for a time his pupil, describes feelingly how he and Moore's dachshund, Fritz, resented this pervasion; but he is surely wrong in thinking that Moore 'could never have liked cats'. It is a curious scene that he describes: the dusty, dilapidated, cat-haunted studio in Holland Lane, Kensington, where were painted those large, sprawling, but anatomically impeccable ladies who appeal so little to modern taste. The younger man once made a determined effort to eliminate the cats. He rummaged behind pictures and canvasses in quest of 'coy or morose specimens', and when he thought the field was clear he shut the door with a bang and determined not to open the low window giving on the leads.

Bump! A heavy object fell from the ceiling, smearing a long streak down my canvas and landing at my feet. 'Pr-r-row,' said the object, regarding me malevolently out of evil yellow eyes. It was a new cat— fallen through the skylight.[5]

In Egypt and in Rome the cat was regarded as being in one way or another a valuable ally to the cultivator, but it remained for Charles Darwin to point out that the size of the purple clover crop depended on the number of cats in the vicinity. The chain of causation is thus unwound. The more cats, the fewer field-mice; the fewer field-mice, the more bumble-bees; the more bumble-bees, the more abundant the purple clover fertilized by them—and, consequently, the more contented the live-stock which feed upon the flowers.

There seems always to have been a curious indifference on the part of many cat-owners as to the naming of their cats. Even the most abject cur is seldom left anonymous: but anyone who glances back over these pages cannot fail to be struck by the number of well-fostered cats who have had to answer to the call of 'Puss', or 'Kitty', or 'Gib', or 'Tom'. Even Pierre Loti, that impassioned catman, confessed that he could never think of an adult she-cat as anything but *'Moumoutte'* and a kitten as anything but *'Mimi'*. An adult male cat did not come into the picture.

On his return from one of his spells of active service with the French navy in Far Eastern waters he found a young Angora cat with a rich coat pied black-and-white established upon the red drawing-room carpet in his widowed mother's Breton home, watched lovingly by Maman and Tante Claire in their deep weeds. He picked up *Moumoutte Blanche* with both his hands, 'paying her those little courtesies which make any

Pierre Loti, (1850-1923). Loti was a French naval officer and novelist, later better known for his exotic novels.

cat decide at once that here is a human being whose caresses may be welcomed graciously'. Thenceforth they were friends.

*Moumoutte Blanche* kept the two old ladies amused during the long winter months when the man of the family was far away. She left flecks of white fur on their sable knees, she leapt into their sacred work-basket and snarled the balls of wool or skeins of silk which lived there. In May she was wont to depart on little jaunts 'not always allowed for as they might have been in the austere circles where her destiny had planted her'. Fastidious, independent, very loving was *Moumoutte Blanche*, uttering a pretty little cry of joy when she returned from one of her 'care-free excursions'.

When she was five years old and at the height of her beauty there was born aboard a Chinese junk in the Bay of Pekin an endearing but far from beautiful *Moumoutte Chinoise* fated to be first her foe and then her friend far away in Brittany. The junk foundered and the little cat, mad with fright, leapt aboard Loti's ship. Seeing what a wan and wispy creature she was, he promptly gave orders that she was to be fed.

> Humbly and gratefully she accepted my attentions. I can see her still, advancing slowly towards this unhoped-for repast, stretching out first one paw and then the other, her light-coloured eyes fixed all the while on me to make sure that she was not deceived, that it was really for *her*.

At first he was reluctant to adopt her; but quietly and persuasively she adopted him. He carried her to the lower deck and handed her over to the crew but, still fixing her eyes on his, she walked meekly and purposefully back to his cabin and installed herself there. His servant aided and abetted her by bringing a cushioned basket to serve as a couch and pushing it under the bed; beside it he thoughtfully placed one of his Captain's large Chinese plates filled with sand—'*detail qui me glaça d'effroi*', wrote Loti, looking back at the remembered scene.

For several months she remained politely within the limits of her couch and her circle of sand. Then one day as he sat writing at his narrow desk he became aware that she was creeping timidly towards him. When she was almost near enough to touch his leg she sat up, curved her tail round her hind-paws and uttered a very sweet little cry, gazing up into his face as she did so. He now had a good look at her. She was the colour of a wild rabbit, with tiger-stripes. Her neck and face were white, her golden eyes had an oriental upward slant at the outer corners, her ears were large and bat-like. For the first time he let his hand fall on her head. That it seemed was what she sought: not food or drink, but a little affection.

Presently she jumped on his knee where she sat for some time, making herself as small and as light as possible, and always watching him anxiously.

What was to be done with this nervous creature, whom the sound of a storm at sea or the noise of the ship's guns frightened so much? Of course she could not be taken home to France. Never would *Moumoutte Blanche* tolerate her presence.

But when her master returned to Brittany, he took her with him. *Madame Moumoutte Blanche* was in great beauty; poor *Madame Moumoutte Chinoise* made a deplorable impression. Even kind Tante Claire was fain to call her 'hideous'.

*Moumoutte Chinoise* was not formally introduced to the Angora. Efforts were made to keep them apart at first: but they met by chance in the kitchen and a battle royal ensued. Fur flew; piercing cries filled the room. But when Loti rescued the quivering Chinese cat and gathered her into his arms a strange thing happened. The Angora, realizing that the intruder belonged to her master accepted the fact that she must do her

Pierre Loti with *Madame Moumoutte Chinoise*, an impressionist painting by Henri Rousseau.

no harm. They never fought again, though for a time they would 'pass each other by, very contemptuous, very correct'.

In the end they became firm friends. The Chinese cat, beautified by a happy life, became in her own way almost as decorative as the Angora. They kissed every morning; they sat on the same chair; when either had a litter of kittens, the other helped to care for them. It was tacitly understood, however, that *Moumoutte Blanche* was Tante Clair's special pet and *Moumoutte Chinoise* Pierre Loti's.

The two *Moumouttes* died within a short time of each other, but *Moumoutte Chinoise* nearly broke her master's heart by creeping away to die alone, he never knew where. Her friend also crept away, but returned at the last to end her days on a bed with a rose-coloured quilt of which she was particularly fond. One morning Loti found her dead, and asked as so many people have done—including Mrs Carlyle with her dog Nero—'*Où était passé ce que j'avais vu luire à travers ses yeux de mourante? La petite flamme inquiète de dedans, où était elle allée?*'[6]

Tante Claire and her Angora provided yet another—and a charming—example of the immemorial association of elderly ladies with cats. The even more ancient link between the cat and the church or temple was forged anew in 1912 when Mr Richards the Verger of St Mary Redcliffe, Bristol, found in that church (described by Queen Elizabeth as the finest parish church in her realm) a handsome tabby stray which remained in or near the sacred spot for fifteen years, and, under the honourable title of the Church Cat, became famous far beyond the walls of its native city.

In warm weather the Church Cat slept in the churchyard; in the winter, in the boiler-room. For his meals he repaired regularly to the Verger's house, but the rest of his time was spent within the sacred walls. Mr E. Richards, the Verger, son of the cat's discoverer, writes to me that the animal, while very active in the churchyard, was very dignified in the church itself.

> He would wander round even when a service was in progress, and during the sermon you might find him resting on the lap of one of the congregation. He would sometimes wander through the chancel between the choir-stalls. The boys and the gentlemen of the choir were not disturbed by his presence.

His portrait appeared in the *Bristol Times* and the *Daily Mirror*, and the caption of the latter reminds the reader that no other cat had heard

*Above left:* Tom the church cat.

*Above right:* St Mary Redcliffe tombstone.

so many sermons. On St Thomas's Day, 1927, he died, full of years and honours, much lamented by the Verger and his family, and by a large circle of admirers. The Vicar of that date gave permission for his interment in the churchyard; his successor authorized the placing of a neat stone upon the little grave with this simple inscription:

THE CHURCH CAT
1912-1927

> There was a kind curate of Kew,
> Who kept a large cat in a pew,
> Where he taught it each week Alphabetical Greek,
> But it never got further than 'mu'

But let us not talk of graves and epitaphs when bidding farewell to this motley pageant of the cat-tribe. The cat in contemporary literature would fill a whole chapter, perhaps even a whole book: and nobody would meet all the examples which nearly everybody would expect to meet. I should like to linger over Margaret Willy's white cat, for whom she wrote so haunting a lament; and Arundell Esdaile's British Museum cat, a formidable fellow; and Alfred Noyes's cat who looked 'with wide unblinking stare' but never saw the King:

The Cat who would learn no Greek but μυ'

The cat who would learn no Greek. *Punch*

She only saw a two-legged creature there
Who in due time might have tit-bits to fling.

I would fain record (if it be still unrecorded) the proposition that
'Dogs looks up to you, and cats looks down on you, but pigs is equals';
although the friend who first quoted it to me cannot now remember
whence it came.

The cat-procession looks like re-forming, and setting off again, and
if it were permitted to do so it would become too populous and stretch
too far. Let me end therefore with a little poem of only nine lines which
will remind every cat-lover of his favourite, irrespective of the colour of
its fur.

A white cat stretches itself in the sun
Beneath some jasmine sprays
That cast a pattern against the shutters.
His eyes are slits, and slanted
Like a Chinese Buddha's.
He turns round, then sleeps again;
The green leaves
Cast their design on his white fur.
O sun, giver of life and of shadows.[7]

# Endnotes

## Chapter 1

1   She sometimes also carries slung upon her left wrist what looks like a serviceable shopping-basket.
2   Because it corresponds to the true Libyan cat and is of the kind found in the great cat-cemetery at Bubastis.
3   *Proc. Zoo. Soc.*, 121 (June, 1951).
4   *Archives du Muséum d'Histoire Naturelle de Lyons*, 1907. Tome VIII.
5   Lortet and Gaillard, *op. cit.*
6   Illustrated by Lortet and Gaillard, *op. cit.*
7   Archdeacon Coxall's translation, 1722.
8   Coxall's translation.

## Chapter 2

1   This element also impressed those two modern masters of the macabre, Dr M. R. James and Algernon Blackwood.
2   From the *Thesaurus Palaeohibernicus*, translated by Whitley and Stokes, Volume II.
3   Some authorities say that a Gib or Gyb cat was a neuter. The gender of the pronouns used with the compound substantive does not give us a clue. For example, Gib is masculine in the Fable of the *Uplandis Mouse* and the *Burgis Mouse*, feminine in the farce of *Gammer Gurton's Needle*. Perhaps the original sex of the animal is thus indicated.

4 How—or by whom—was his skin burnt? Neither here nor later do I propose to dwell upon the horrible cruelties long practised upon his kind. The old simile 'like a scalded cat' has uncomfortable implications.

5 In a fourteenth-century religious treatise, *The Again-bite of Inwit*, we read that the devil plays often with the soul 'as doth the Cat with the Mouse'.

6 This is not invariably true. I have known a 'wel-fostred' cat who desired a mouse neither as a plaything nor as a *plat-du-jour* and I have been told of one who, having sat down by mistake upon a mouse, rose up with a shriek of alarm.

7 Roving and revelling, with vocal accompaniment.

8 *Piers Plowman B.* Prologue: II. 165-81.

9 Walter Scott, *Tales of a Grandfather.*

10 Stomach.

11 See page xxx for Robert Burns' use of the name 'Bawdrins' for a cat.

12 Grasped. Compare Hamlet's 'Up, sword, and know thou a more horrid hent'.

13 Merry.

14 Hide and seek.

15 Partition wall.

16 Stomach.

17 Without.

18 Without.

19 In his autobiography, *Looking Back* (1958).

20 A comedy by Chapman, Marston and Jonson.

21 Alfred Noyes. *Tales of the Mermaid Tavern.* VIII. *Flos Mercatorum.*

# Chapter 3

1 *Catus* is post-classical Latin for a male cat.

2 Lover of learning.

3 One possessed of understanding.

4 Slightly anglicized for the benefit of the Sassenach reader.

5 Four other 'witches'.

6 Most of these hangings are in the possession of the National Trust at Oxburgh Hall, Norfolk, but the cat panel was sold separately at Sotheby's in October, 1957.

## Chapter 4    FEB 0.5 2016

1   See Dr George Lincoln Burr's *Narratives of the Witchcraft Cases: 1648-1706*.
2   The rumbling stone, apparently, not the music.
3   Translated by John Florio.
4   See 'The Female Friend' by the Rev. Cornelius Whur, in *The Stuffed Owl* by D. B. Wyndham Lewis.
5   The word means a large flake of copper or gold. She may have been a tortoiseshell or a ginger cat.
6   The Sixth Satire of the Second Book.
7   See Southey's poem quoted on page XX.

## Chapter 5

1   See Chapter 2, page XX.
2   Wyndham Ketton-Cremer: *Thomas Gray*.
3   Second son of the First Duke of Argyll. Succeeded his brother as 3rd Duke, 1743.
4   At the Strawberry Hill sale in 1840 the vase was bought by the Lord Derby of the day. It is at Knowsley.

## Chapter 6

1   It was apparently a tallboy, yet not so 'tall' that the top-drawer was beyond the reach of her leap.
2   Mrs Sarah Austin, according to Professor George Saintsbury. She also translated Ranke's *History of the Popes* and F. Carove's *Story without an End*.
3   According to Dr Brewer in the *Dictionary of Phrase and Fable* the proverb was suggested by the fact that Cheshire cheese used at one time to be made in moulds shaped like the face of a smiling cat.
4   *The Holy Grail*.
5   Graham Robertson, *Time Was*.
6   Pierre Loti, *Le Livre de la Pitié et de la Mort*.
7   From *St Albans and other Poems* by Theodora Roscoe (1953).